THE AR

THE ART OF SPEECH

A HANDBOOK OF ELOCUTION

BY

KATHLEEN RICH

LICENTIATE IN ELOCUTION OF THE GUILDHALL SCHOOL OF MUSIC
(WITH HONOURS)
MEMBER OF THE ROYAL SOCIETY OF TEACHERS

FOURTH EDITION

GRESHAM BOOKS

First published August 1932
Second edition September 1946
Reprinted 1953, 1959
Revised Third Edition 1967
Revised Fourth Edition 1979

© *Estate of Kathleen Rich, 1979*

ISBN 0 905418 38 7

Gresham Books
Unwin Brothers Limited
The Gresham Press
Old Woking, Surrey
England

Printed and bound in England by
Staples Printers Rochester Limited
at The Stanhope Press.

TO
MY PUPILS

FOREWORD

BY GRETA DOUGLAS
Fellow of Trinity College, London

Oral communication is, more than ever before, a vital necessity of modern life.

Kathleen Rich has treated the subject of correct, expressive speech in a beautifully simple manner yet with a breadth and thoroughness that will make it a first-class guide for teachers and students alike.

The section on breathing is exceptionally clear, and I could wish that schools everywhere would benefit from her words of wisdom on this subject. Indeed it is a sad fact that too many of us are in need of such inspiring encouragement (for health, mental alertness, and for vocal power and colour too) as Miss Rich has given us.

If only for the chapter on breathing this book should be in the hands of all who deal with the spoken word, both school teachers and speech specialists.

NOTE TO FOURTH EDITION

This latest edition of *The Art of Speech* has been revised and updated by Susan Ford, F.G.S.M., L.G.S.M., Professor of Speech and Drama at the Guildhall School of Music and Drama. Revisions have been incorporated which reflect changes of emphasis and technique since the late Kathleen Rich prepared the Third Edition in 1967. The publishers wish to thank Professor Ford for her assistance in the preparation of this new edition.

PREFACE

WHEN I BEGAN the revision of this book, realizing that the term ' Elocution ' is somewhat out of favour, I tried to avoid its use. Soon this proved impossible. There is no other term with quite the same meaning. ' Speech and Drama ' is the best alternative, but as will be seen, was, here, not always suitable.

When George Bernard Shaw put into the mouth of Professor Higgins the dictum that by transforming some one's speech one transformed his personality, he propounded a doctrine the truth of which has been proved time and again. The metamorphosis may not be as dramatic as that of Eliza Doolittle, but it may be very striking all the same.

Many students have come to me because they have been told by their employers that they are hindered from promotion by their poor speech. One Civil Servant spoke through clenched teeth, without moving his lips, to such a degree that he was literally incomprehensible. After months of really hard work his speech greatly improved, and the promotion was gained.

Recently I was told of a boy who left school with a brilliant scholastic record. He applied for a post, was asked to write a paper; on the result of which he was called for an interview. He passed the paper with over 90% marks. The interview he failed. Application for another post produced exactly the same result—except that he gained an even higher percentage on the paper-work. The knowledge was his; the ability to communicate verbally, disastrously lacking.

Socially, of course, good speech is very important. All of us know good-looking, well-dressed people, who spoil their pleasing impression as soon as they begin to talk.

I wish to thank most gratefully my friend and former pupil Miss Myrtle Topley, L.G.S.M., A.L.A.M., for her invaluable and generous help throughout the preparation of this book.

CROYDON 1967   KATHLEEN RICH

CONTENTS

CONTENTS

PART II

POLISHING AND USING THE MIRROR

Speak the speech, I pray you, as I pronounced it to you, trippingly on the tongue: but if you mouth it, as many of your players do, I had as lief the town-crier spoke my lines. Nor do not saw the air too much with your hand, thus, but use all gently; for in the very torrent, tempest, and, as I may say, the whirlwind of passion, you must acquire and beget a temperance that may give it smoothness. O, it offends me to the soul to hear a robustious periwig-pated fellow tear a passion to tatters, to very rags, to split the ears of the groundlings who for the most part are capable of nothing but inexplicable dumb-shows and noise: I would have such a fellow whipped for o'er-doing Termagant; it out-herods Herod: pray you, avoid it.

Be not too tame neither, but let your own discretion be your tutor: suit the action to the word, the word to the action; with this special observance, that you o'erstep not the modesty of nature: for anything so overdone is from the purpose of playing, whose end, both at the first and now, was and is, to hold, as 'twere, the mirror up to nature; to show virtue her own feature, scorn her own image, and the very age and body of the time his form and pressure. Now this overdone, or come tardy off, though it make the unskilful laugh, cannot but make the judicious grieve; the censure of the which one must in your allowance o'erweigh a whole theatre of others. O, there be players that I have seen play, and heard others praise, and that highly, not to speak it profanely, that, neither having the accent of Christians nor the gait of Christian, pagan, nor man, have so strutted and bellowed that I have thought some of nature's journeymen had made men and not made them well, they imitated humanity so abominably.

O, reform it altogether. And let those that play your clowns speak no more than is set down for them; for there be of them that will themselves laugh, to set on some quantity of barren spectators to laugh too; though, in the mean time, some necessary question of the play be then to be considered: that's villainous, and shows a most pitiful ambition in the fool that uses it. Go, make you ready.

Hamlet

INTRODUCTION

IT IS THE writer's belief that the watchword of every student of Speech and Drama should be, ' to hold the mirror up to Nature '. As to Hamlet's players three hundred years ago, so to us who desire to ' speak the speech ' to-day, these words of Shakespeare offer goodly counsel : ' o'erstep not the modesty of nature.'

In this book an attempt is made to show that perfect speech is essentially natural. Nature has given to each of us the materials necessary for the making of our mirror. She has planned it all—the making, the polishing, and finally the using of the mirror—but it is for us to carry out the work. We can, and very often do, omit to use the materials, and leave it all alone. Or we use them in our own way, and not in Nature's, so that, if we make a mirror at all, it is not as clear as it should be, or it is one of those which distort the image they reflect. For Nature's laws are very plain, and hers is the right way. If we refuse to learn her lessons, or to work on her advice, then we must take the consequences. At best, we must be content with less than perfection, for it is very sure that we shall never reach that goal.

It seems strange that we should have to learn to be natural, but so it certainly is. Clearly, we cannot reflect the natural by being, ourselves, artificial, and, unless we have patiently studied naturalness, nervousness will have its way with us, making us stiff, awkward—indeed, unnatural.

The Theory of Speech has not been invented, and applied, as it were, from without. The Laws are the result of the observations of experts, who have noted our natural inflections, natural pauses, gestures and manner of speech generally, and from their observations have evolved the Theory of Speech and Drama. We have not to study some abstruse subject, but simply to learn how to apply our natural means of expression to our studied speech.

xi

So this book is divided into two parts. In the first, the materials are described, and the manner of their use. First, the backing of the mirror, upon which all depends— a method of breathing. Second, the glass, which ranks next in importance to the backing—the voice, and its production. Third, the framework, which holds it all together—the power of speech. Last, the quicksilver, which gives the life, the power of reflection—our means of expression ; our chance ' to show virtue her own feature, scorn her own image, and the very age and body of the time, his form and pressure '.

The second part of the book deals with the polishing and the using of the mirror, through our study and rendering of various types of work—verse and prose, character study, reading aloud, and so on.

And another point. We must not imagine, having made our mirror, polished it, and effectively used it, that our work is ended. We shall have constantly and tirelessly to work to preserve our mirror always clear and flawless. Only frequent use and thoughtful care can ever keep it so.

PART I

MAKING THE MIRROR

CHAPTER I

THE BACKING OF THE MIRROR : BREATHING

WE HAVE LIKENED the study and practice of the art of speech to the making and using of a mirror. The first element of speech, the backing of our mirror, is a method of breathing. The breathing apparatus is wonderfully constructed, and its operation, including the effect of oxygen on the blood-stream, the various chemical changes which take place in the contents of the lungs during respiration, and so on, forms a most interesting study. There is no need, however, for the elocution student to learn more than the construction of the apparatus and its correct functioning ; so much being necessary, in many cases, before an effortless, and finally, unconscious control over the breath can be gained.

It seems extraordinary that men and women, boys and girls alike, should need to be taught to breathe correctly, but such is undoubtedly the case. Any teacher of physical training, voice production, or singing, must have the same experience. The great majority of people misuse their breathing apparatus. The lower ribs, where the greatest degree of expansion should take place, and the diaphragm, are scarcely used at all, so that too small a quantity of air is inspired at each breath. In consequence, both adults and children are starved for air, and appalling numbers of them suffer from adenoids, catarrh, and all kinds of affections of the nose and throat, to say nothing of the fact that they are constantly below par, and ready to pick up any infection with which they may come into contact. And the evil does not end there. A London specialist once said, that ninety per cent of the ailments with which patients came to him were traceable, directly or indirectly, to faulty methods of breathing. He was referring, not only to conditions which would obviously be caused in this way, such as affections of the chest, nose, and throat, but to diseases which many people would never connect with breathing at all. Indigestion, for instance, would appear to have very little to do with the functioning of the breathing apparatus, but, if we consider the necessity for the bloodstream to be charged with oxygen before it enters the digestive system, the connection becomes clear enough.

A French doctor, on reaching his ninety-eighth birthday, said that any normally constituted person should be able to live for at least a hundred years. He held that many people kill themselves by sheer laziness—it is too much trouble to breathe deeply, and at each inspiration they breathe only one quart of air instead of the requisite three or four quarts. In this connection, teachers of speech and singing might work with the medical profession much more than they do at present. After operations for adenoids, for instance, children should always be taught to breathe correctly. They have so strongly formed the habit of mouth-breathing, that they still continue to breathe through the mouth after the obstruction in the nasal passages has been removed. Thus, the operation is frequently rendered quite useless, for the adenoids begin to grow again immediately. The only way to prevent this happening is for the sufferer to breathe through the nose. Whether adenoids are the cause of mouth-breathing, or whether they are, as many people believe, the effect of it, is a matter which is worthy of deep consideration.

In the opinion of the present writer, the cause of this almost universal misuse of the breathing apparatus is this : our grandmothers for many generations wore gowns which were tight-laced. These women could not breathe deeply —it was impossible. They were, in consequence, very short of breath, and subject to attacks of faintness and the vapours. But what is far more serious is that they have handed this method of breathing down to their children, who, unless they are taught otherwise, will breathe in just the same unnatural, cramped, top-of-the-lung manner. Whatever may be the cause, the resulting conditions are clear enough, and must be remedied for the health and well-being of the race. The student needs to grasp two facts. One is that it is impossible to over-emphasize the importance of a correct method of breathing ; the other that there can be only one correct method. Nature has given us a delicate and complicated system of bones, muscles, nerves and tissues with which to breathe, and which must be intended to function in one way, and in one way only. There is only one correct method of breathing, just as there is only one way in which the heart can beat. The great difference is, that the beating of the heart is entirely involuntary, whereas we can, once we have understood its working, gain perfect control over the breathing apparatus. Yes, once we have understood its working. It is often argued that a knowledge of the construction and action of the breathing apparatus is unnecessary to the student—indeed, harmful, as it distracts his attention from his performance. But surely, a student who is completely ignorant of the position and functioning of organs over which he is trying to gain control must be working in the dark. He is as one who starts out to find some place which he knows to be not far distant, but of the whereabouts of which he is ignorant. However hard he tries, he may never find his goal, though he may stumble upon it by chance.

It must not be imagined that we have constantly to be thinking about breathing and breath control. Far from it. Once control has been gained it will never be lost. It becomes involuntary, and we are as unconscious of it as of the way in which we walk and talk.

THE BREATHING APPARATUS

This comprises :

1. **The Abdominal Muscles,** which remain still during inspiration for voice or action, and which, by their contraction (the abdominal press), aid the other muscles in controlling the outward flow of breath. Thus, the abdominal wall is slightly drawn in during expiration.

2. **The Diaphragm**—a large muscle, shaped rather like an open umbrella. It divides the body in two, forming the floor of the chest and the roof of the abdomen. It is joined at the back to the spine, round the sides to the lower ribs, and in front to the breast-bone, or sternum. During inspiration it contracts and flattens itself (*see* Fig. 1), thus increasing enormously the capacity of the chest downward. Its function is most important.

3. **The Thorax, or Chest.** This consists of the bony ' cage ' containing principally the heart, the thyroid and other glands, the big blood vessels, the lungs, and the bronchial tubes, which lead from the lungs to the trachea, or wind-pipe.

4. **The Lungs.** There are two lungs, the left and the right. They are conical in shape, with the apex upward, and concave at the base. They rest on the diaphragm, and in substance resemble a sponge. They are formed of very elastic tissue, and contain hundreds of thousands of tiny air cells and passages. In formation, the air passages are rather like inverted trees.

5. **The Intercostal Muscles**—(*inter*, between ; *costa*, rib). There are two sets of these muscles, one which draws the ribs upward and outward with a ' bucket-handle ' movement during inspiration, and the other which restores them to their former position during expiration.

6. **The Bronchial Tubes,** through which the breath passes from the lungs to

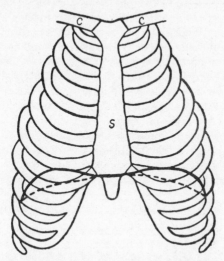

FIG. I. THE THORAX, OR CHEST, FROM THE FRONT

This diagram shows the Collar-bones, C; the Sternum, or Breastbone, S; and the Ribs. Of the twelve pairs of ribs only eleven are visible, as the last pair is too short to be seen from the front. The position of the summit of the Diaphragm after expiration is roughly indicated by the heavy black line; and after inspiration by the dotted line. In very deep, and in laboured breathing, the movement of the diaphragm is, of course, more pronounced.

7. **The Trachea,** or Wind-pipe, which can be felt in the neck, and which continues up to

8. **The Larynx,** or Voice-box.

9. **The Pharynx.** This is the passage between the larynx and the cavities of

10. **The Nose and Mouth.** Except during phonation, nose breathing is always desirable.

Respiration, the act of breathing, consists of

    (*a*) Inspiration—breathing in.

    (*b*) Expiration—breathing out.

Normally an adult completes, on an average, seventeen respirations per minute. When one is breathing in repose, the following involuntary movement takes place :

The diaphragm contracts and flattens, and so descends upon the organs (the liver, etc.) immediately beneath it. The front abdominal wall moves outward. Displacement of the organs is allowed by the protrusion of the abdominal wall. The lungs are expanded, particularly at their base. There is very little movement of the ribs. There is a considerable pause between respirations. Breathing in repose is much more diaphragmatic than breathing for voice or action. During expiration, the organs return to their former position. (' *Repose* ' *means resting, not necessarily sleeping.*)

THE CORRECT METHOD OF BREATHING

The only satisfactory method of breathing for voice is the **Intercostal-Diaphragmatic** method, by which the chest is enlarged to its fullest extent, its size being increased vertically, transversely, and in its diameter from before backward.

The front abdominal wall is controlled and remains still during inspiration. The descent of the diaphragm is less marked than in breathing in repose, because the rigidity of the abdominal wall prevents any displacement of the organs immediately beneath the diaphragm. The ribs swing outward at the back and sides as well as in front. The breast-bone moves forward. The lungs are expanded in every direction, though the expansion upward, compared with the movement downward and outward, is negligible.

During expiration, the front abdominal wall is slightly drawn inward (the abdominal press). The diaphragm returns slowly to its former position. The ribs are held outward by the intercostal muscles until the breath is partly exhausted, and then very slowly allowed to relapse.

In this way complete control is obtained over the outgoing column of air, for the chest cavity remains enlarged, and the only pressure comes upward from the diaphragm, so that the flow of breath is kept quite steady.

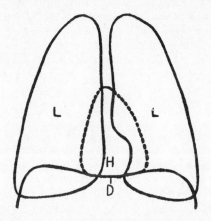

FIG. 2.   THE RELATIVE POSITIONS OF THE HEART, H; LUNGS, L; AND
DIAPHRAGM, D

Where the heart is covered by the lungs, it is indicated by the dotted line.   Owing to the domed shape of the diaphragm, and the fact that the lungs are concave at the base, they appear to overlap the diaphragm in front.   It is the summit of the dome of the diaphragm which is indicated.   The covering of the heart is joined to the diaphragm.

It is a help to children to think of pressing a tube of cold cream as an illustration of this method.   If the tube is pressed gently from the end first (the abdominal press), the cream flows out in a steady stream.   If though, the tube is pressed higher up (when the ribs are allowed to relapse too soon), the cream comes out in lumps, and very unevenly.

It should be borne in mind that the base of the lung fills with air before the apex.   We fill the lungs with air just as we fill a glass with water, from below upward. And it is a mistake to suppose that the chest cavity expands to make room for incoming air. Quite the reverse. The movements of respiration are involuntary, and when air enters the lungs, it is to fill what would otherwise be the vacuum created by their expansion. The greatest expansion takes place all round the body, just below the level of the lower end of the breast bone. This can be felt plainly.

The control of the breath during phonation must be exercised by the muscles of the chest and abdomen. To check its flow by tightening the muscles of the throat is dangerous in the extreme to the beauty and well-being of the voice.

NOSE AND MOUTH BREATHING

As has already been pointed out, nose breathing should always be used, except for voice. Nature has provided us, in the nose, with an instrument which warms and filters the air we breathe. During speech or song, however, there is seldom time to take in a sufficient quantity of air quickly enough through the comparatively small nasal passages. Another most important fact is that during nose breathing the Soft Palate[1] is lowered, and sometimes does not rise sufficiently rapidly, on the commencement of phonation. This causes nasal or 'plummy' tone. During mouth breathing the soft palate is raised toward the back wall of the pharynx, and the mouth passage is, therefore, open and ready for voice.

On the other hand, teachers and others who have to use their voices for many hours each day, often in stuffy, ill-ventilated rooms, sometimes find it helpful to take in breath as often as possible during speech, through the nose. With practice, this is quite easy to do, and brings relief from tiredness and strain. In speech of this description, it is possible to make pauses in which it is practicable to breathe through the nose, taking a quick mouth breath before beginning to speak, and nasal tone need not result if care is taken to gain control over the soft palate.

[1] See Appendix

Some people, children in particular, experience difficulty in breathing quietly through the mouth. As an exercise, they should breathe through the mouth during practice; and exercises for mouth breathing, beginning with a slow breath, and gradually increasing the quickness of the intake, are helpful. Moreover, they should never attempt long phrases, and should practise breath-control exercises, as a large part of the trouble is lack of control. (*See exercises at end of Chapter I and on p.* 17.)

INCORRECT METHODS OF BREATHING

A method of breathing for voice which has largely been taught in the past is the **Abdominal Method.** This is an exaggeration of the breathing in repose which has been described. The abdominal wall is protruded, and the diaphragm allowed to descend to its lowest. It is impossible for the chest to expand properly if the diaphragm is very much flattened, for it is attached to the lower ribs, and prevents their rising. This is bad, not only because it is unsightly, but because, the ribs being only partly expanded, the quantity of air inspired is small. There is very little control over the outgoing column of air, as the only muscles employed to any appreciable extent are the abdominal muscles and the diaphragm.

Another method, which is almost invariably seen in schools when the children are told to ' take a deep breath,' is the **Clavicular**, or **Collar-bone, Method.** This is the direct opposite to the abdominal method. Abdominal is too low, clavicular too high. The shoulders are raised, and the upper ribs so drawn up that the diaphragm is unable to descend. This greatly increases susceptibility to chills and colds.

These methods are among the most common causes of tremolo, of shortness of breath, of breathy tone, and lack of resonance.

Nature cannot have meant us to breathe by either of these methods, for in both cases we are expecting organs to do work for which they are obviously not intended, and are neglecting the proper expansion at the base of the lungs, which we can see for ourselves is the part of the breathing apparatus designed to play a most important role in feeding the body with air.

BREATHING EXERCISES

1. Relax.   Place hands over lower ribs.   Concentrate on this point.   Breathe OUT, drawing abdominal muscles IN.   Breathe IN.   Feel expansion of lower chest.   Repeat slowly six times.

2. Repeat, beginning slowly, increasing to a rapid pace.

3. Take a deep breath, and hum it out on any easy note. Feel vibration on lips.

4. Take a deep breath.   Count aloud, or say a nursery rhyme as many times as possible in one breath.

Breathe through the nose throughout.

When attempting to take a deep breath, never draw in the abdominal muscles.   The abdominal press controls the flow of air during *expiration*.

CHAPTER II

THE GLASS OF THE MIRROR: THE VOICE

IF WE EXAMINE the elements of speech one by one, we shall find that the next to Breathing, in order of importance, is certainly Voice. It is, so to speak, the glass of our mirror.

Nature, it seems, is singularly capricious in her distribution of speaking-voices. Here, ' a voice like the drip of a honey-comb '; there, one which is just the reverse. There is a general impression that voices are like faces; they belong to us and we must put up with them. There never was a more mistaken idea. The possession of a beautiful voice is within the reach of any normally constituted person who will take the trouble to learn the technique of voice-production, and will give some time to painstaking practice. One's voice is not a matter of the caprice of Nature, but of the use or misuse of the vocal mechanism. Misuse of the apparatus must, sooner or later, produce one inevitable result—an unsatisfactory voice. Voices which are harsh, unpleasing, which tire easily, and the possessors of which are subject to attacks of Clergyman's Throat and Tonsilitis, are so because they are wrongly produced. Lack of head resonance, the incorrect placing of the voice, any tendency to tighten muscles (even if they appear to have no connection with the speaking apparatus), will produce such results. The correction of the fault will work apparent miracles.

So many people fail to realize the tremendous importance of opening the mouth, and relaxing all the muscles of the mouth and throat during speech as well as during song. It is fairly generally understood that the mouth and throat must be well open when one is singing, but few people fully realize the effect that the *free* opening of the mouth, and the relaxation of the muscles which this entails, has upon the speaking-voice. Of course, the mouth should not be opened unnaturally wide. It is the freedom, the looseness and flexibility of the muscles employed which counts. This is of paramount importance. And here it must be emphasized that the student should aim at relaxation of *every muscle in the body* during phonation. Each member is so true and important a part of the whole, that tenseness and rigidity of any part of the body, will immediately affect the vocal muscles, and through them, the voice.

(*Some relaxation exercises will be found on p.* 49.)

The correct shaping of the mouth for vowel sounds has also its effect upon the voice, partly, no doubt, because it is impossible to keep any muscle connected with the lips and mouth rigid, when the sounds are properly formed; and partly because the production is naturally more forward when certain sounds such as ' oo ' and ' aw ' are correctly shaped, and this has its effect upon all the vowel sounds.

Now, what is Voice? Voice, like all other sounds, is caused by the vibration of air. The vibration in this case is set up by the column of air as it leaves the lungs through the wind-pipe, coming into contact with the **Vocal Bands, or Cords.** The term ' vocal bands ' is used throughout these notes because of its familiarity, but, as a matter of fact, neither ' band ' nor ' cord ' is a good name, for both convey the idea of a thread stretched across the voice-box. ' Vocal Folds ' would perhaps be better, for the vocal cords are actually folds of elastic tissue attached to the sides of the larynx, with their inner edges free.

The **Larynx,** or **Voice-box,** is a structure formed of cartilage, which hangs below the tongue-bone, and at the top of the wind-pipe. The largest of the cartilages which form the ' box ' is the Thyroid Cartilage, which is attached by a membrane to the tongue-bone, and further supported by muscles. It is the front surface of this cartilage, better known as ' Adam's Apple ', which can be felt in the neck. If the fingers are laid over the ' apple ' during phonation, its vibration and freedom of movement can plainly be felt. Below the thyroid, and next to it in size, is the Cricoid Cartilage, which supports two most

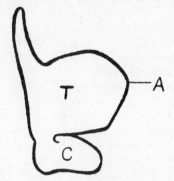

FIG. 3. THE LARYNX, VIEWED FROM THE SIDE

This shows the Thyroid Cartilage, T; its front surface, ' Adam's Apple ', A; and the Cricoid Cartilage, C.

important structures, the Arytenoid Cartilages. It is to these that the vocal bands are attached at the back. In

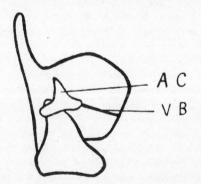

FIG. 4. THE INTERIOR OF THE BISECTED LARYNX

The Cartilages in Fig. 3 are shown; also the Arytenoid Cartilage, AC; and the Vocal Bands, VB.

front, they are joined to the thyroid cartilage. Above the vocal bands are two folds of mucous membrane, the False

Vocal Bands, which serve as a protection to the true bands, but have no function in the production of voice. Below the cricoid cartilage, the larynx joins the trachea. The chink between the vocal bands through which the air passes, is called the Glottis. The glottis is protected from above by a kind of lid, the Epiglottis, which closes the air-passage during swallowing. As the food-pipe is behind the wind-pipe, all food taken has to pass over the top of the trachea. Here is the danger of 'speaking with your mouth full'. The epiglottis is raised to allow breath to pass, and the food quite literally 'goes down the wrong way', entering the air passage, whence it must be dislodged by coughing, or by even more violent measures.

The most delicate and wonderful adjustment takes place in the larynx when the voice is used. The arytenoid cartilages are movable—they swivel round on their base, and so bring the vocal bands close together for voice. At the same time, muscles cause the arytenoid cartilages to tilt forward or backward to a greater or lesser degree, so determining the tension of the vocal bands. As the pitch of the voice depends upon this tension, the importance of the work done by these muscles and cartilages may readily be understood. When the voice is not in use, the vocal bands are drawn back by the action of muscles upon the arytenoids to the sides of the larynx. If this were not so, we should vocalize with every breath.

When the column of air leaving the lungs comes into contact with the vocal bands, they are made to vibrate. Their vibration passes to the whole column of air, from the base of the lungs to the top of the head, which thus becomes voice. The fact that the whole column of air vibrates can be demonstrated by placing the hands over any part of the air passages, including the lungs, during phonation.

Although the function of the larynx is of the greatest importance, it must not be imagined that it alone constitutes the voice-producing apparatus. Voice, when it leaves the larynx, is very small and thin in tone. It lacks that most vital quality—**Resonance.** It is obvious that the vibration set up by anything so small as the vocal bands, which are less than one inch in length, must be but slight. The tone produced by drawing the bow across the strings of a violin would be very poor, were it not for the vibration set up in the body of the fiddle and in the air within it. The same thing applies, and to a far greater degree, to voice. The whole column of air certainly vibrates, but the most important resonance chambers are in the head, mouth and throat, probably because these are mostly formed of bony substance, while the lungs are soft and spongy. In the roof of the mouth we have a perfect natural sounding-board, known as the Hard Palate. The function of the Soft Palate, which greatly affects the shape of the mouth cavity and the quality of the voice, is so important that it will be described separately later. The passage between the nose and the larynx—the Pharynx— which lies at the back of the mouth cavity, forms another resonating chamber. Above the pharynx are the Nasal Cavities, which are universally recognized as having a most important part to play in the production of voice, and above these again, cavities called the Head Sinuses, the influence of which has been the cause of a good deal of controversy among professors of voice-production. One thing, at any rate, is certain. Concentration upon these cavities of the head and nose is of the greatest value to a student in gaining resonance, and the fact that vibration does take place in the head cavities can be proved by placing the hand over the top of the head during phonation. The importance of the part played by the nasal cavities in producing resonance may be demonstrated by speaking with closed nostrils. To some extent the same effect of deadness of tone will result as is heard when one is suffering from a cold in the head. Loudness may be obtained by shouting, but the tone cannot fail to be unpleasant, and the effect upon the voice, injurious. Concentration upon the larynx is absolutely fatal, for it is bound to lead to tenseness and constriction of the muscles.

Now to consider the **Soft Palate.** This is an organ of speech and voice-production, with regard to the function of which the ideas of most students are extremely hazy. They realize clearly enough that it operates together with the tongue to form certain consonant sounds, but they overlook its other function, which, indeed, is far more important. When the soft palate is lowered, and approximates with the tongue, it closes the passage into the mouth, so that the voice is either completely stopped, and released when the contact of the organs is broken, as in ' g ', or directed into the nasal cavities, as in ' ng '. When the back of the tongue is lowered, and the soft palate moderately raised, the passage into the mouth *and* the nose is open. It is possible completely to shut off the nasal passage by raising the soft palate so that it touches the back wall of the pharynx. The influence of this organ upon voice-production is enormous. Unless it responds quickly, and is raised at once upon the commencement of any sounds other than the nasal and guttural consonants, it seriously interferes with the quality of the voice.[1] The defect caused in this way, and its remedy, will be discussed in the notes on Speech Defects.

It is of the utmost importance that a student of elocution should understand clearly the method of voice-production at which he is aiming. Correct production can be obtained only by directing the voice well forward on to the teeth ridge; by gaining control over the soft palate, and by concentrating upon the cavities of the head, nose and mouth, thus obtaining resonance. The acquirement of perfect breath control is indispensable.

It may be helpful to the student to have before him a tabulated list of the organs employed in the production of voice. They are as follows:

ORGANS OF VOICE-PRODUCTION

1. **The Breathing Apparatus,** which has been described in the chapter on Breathing.

---

[1] Exercise follows at the end of the chapter.

2. **The Larynx,** containing the Vocal Bands.

3. **The Pharynx,** which is the connecting passage between the Larynx and the Mouth and Nose, and an important resonator.

4. **The Resonating Cavities** of the mouth, nose and head.

5. **The Organs of Speech,** in so far as, by their position, they affect the quality of the tone produced.

CARE OF THE VOICE

So much admirable advice has been written elsewhere with regard to vocal hygiene, that it is unnecessary to go deeply into the subject here. Just one or two hints, however, which have been of value to the writer, may be equally valuable to others.

After using your voice in a hot building, be careful to breathe through the nose for at least five minutes after coming out into the cold air. Do not even talk, but keep your mouth closed. Otherwise the shock of the cold air on your throat may lead to a cold, or to loss of voice.

It is unwise, for a similar reason, to drink cold water during or after an evening's work. Before you begin, yes; but not after.

Never suck lozenges, except by doctor's orders. It is fatally easy to form a lozenge habit, which is very bad for your throat. A good gargle, such as a few drops of T.C.P. in warm water, is of infinitely greater value.

Exercise for the Soft Palate

Breathe in and out through the mouth alternately, thus:
In through the nose; out through the mouth.
In through the mouth; out through the nose, and so on.
Begin slowly, and increase to a rapid pace.

If you watch in a mirror the movement of the soft palate, while practising this exercise, you will see how flexibility is increased.

CHAPTER III

THE FRAMEWORK OF THE MIRROR: SPEECH

' Speak the speech, I pray you . . . trippingly on the tongue.'

A CERTAIN GREAT British dramatist, during the preparations for the production of one of his plays, put up an urgent plea to the Director that the cast should be made up of ' articulate beings '.

That is rather significant. It makes one realize more than ever how many actors and actresses forget to consider whether they are articulate beings or not. It is a sad state of affairs, for surely we should be able to look to the Stage to set us an example of our tongue as it should be spoken.

We see on the stage today the reaction from the exaggeration of the old conventions, the stilted, unnatural, ' stagey ' behaviour which held sway some years back. The players are so very anxious to be completely ' natural ', that they never stop to consider whether or not they are intelligible, and, to a great extent, the reciter suffers from the same complaint.

Do let us realize that, if only we will use our speaking apparatus as Nature intends us to use it, we shall be intelligible. It is not natural for us to talk through our clenched teeth, or without moving our lips, or in a languid manner which suggests that it is too much trouble to speak at all. It is most unnatural. We are distorting our speaking apparatus, and can only expect to be rather inarticulate, and to find that our throats are inclined to ache, and our voices to be harsh and unpleasing. Watch a small child speaking, one who has only just learned to speak. See how pliable the lips are, how well open the mouth. There is no strain, no rigidity. That is natural speech.

In order to speak, that is, to utter articulate sounds,

we have to make both vowel and consonant sounds.
Vowels are those sounds which are made by the voice and
shaped by the position of organs of speech. They are
open sounds uninterrupted by any contact of the organs
of speech. (If one sings a long note, and repeatedly alters
the shape of the mouth cavity during phonation, one will
sing a series of different vowel sounds.) Many people are
confused between the five vowels of the English language,
written *a*, *e*, *i*, *o*, *u*, and the eighteen vowel sounds which
are derived from them. They are as follows:

THE VOWEL SOUNDS

Of the eighteen vowel sounds, twelve are monophthongal
(one sound), and six diphthongal (two sounds). During
the speaking or singing of the monophthongals, there is no
change in the position of the organs of speech. The
diphthongals are formed by making one sound, and then,
by changing the shape of the mouth, uniting it with
another.

Monophthongal Vowel Sounds

    1. ă   as in hat.
    2. āh ,, ,, calm.
    3. ă   ,, ,, awaken (the neutral).
    4. āw ,, ,, yawn.
    5. ĕ   ,, ,, egg.
    6. ē   ,, ,, feel.
    7. ēr ,, ,, fern.
    8. ĭ   ,, ,, pit.
    9. ŏ   ,, ,, hot.
  10. ōo ,, ,, moon.
  11. ŭ   ,, ,, hut.
  12. ŏo ,, ,, push.

The monophthongs ee, oo, aw, ah (and possibly ur) are sometimes
classified as 'long', the rest as 'short'. At the same time it must
not be forgotten that it is possible to sustain *any* vowel sound as long as
the breath lasts.

Diphthongal Vowel Sounds

1. $\bar{\text{i}}$ as in light = ah (2) united with $\breve{\text{i}}$ (8).
2. ou ,, ,, house = ah (2) ,, ,, oo (10).
3. oi ,, ,, noise = aw (4) ,, ,, $\breve{\text{i}}$ (8).
4. $\bar{\text{u}}$,, ,, tune = $\breve{\text{i}}$ (8) ,, ,, oo (10).
5. $\bar{\text{a}}$,, ,, stain = eh ,, ,, $\breve{\text{i}}$ (8).
6. $\bar{\text{o}}$,, ,, note = $\bar{\text{o}}$,, ,, oo (10).

A and O differ from the others, as the inital sounds do not occur as monophthongs in English.

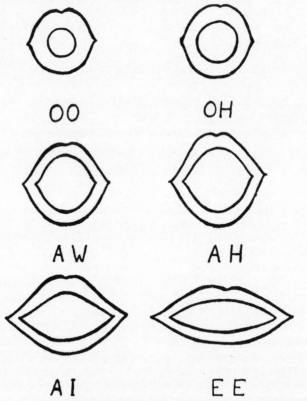

FIG. 5. THE POSITIONS OF THE LIPS FOR THE COMMENCEMENT OF THE PRODUCTION OF VARIOUS VOWEL SOUNDS

It should be noted that the French ' o ' and ' a ' are monophthongal. They are shorter sounds than ours, and have no change of position.

The true production of all vowel sounds depends upon the correct shaping of the mouth. In his book on voice-production the late Dr. Wesley Mills gives an exercise for demonstrating that each vowel sound has its own vocal pitch, which is most valuable for ascertaining that vowel sounds are correctly formed. Shape the mouth cavity for the attack on vowel sounds as follows: oo, oh, aw, ah, ai, ĕ, ĭ, ee (without producing voice). As each sound is shaped, fillip the finger against the cheek, when an ascending scale should result. If the shaping of the mouth is incorrect, the right notes cannot be produced. It is most important that the tongue should lie very low in the mouth for ' oo '. The thin quality so often heard in this sound is the result of the tongue being placed too high in the mouth, quite as often as it is the result of the lips being insufficiently rounded.

The neutral vowel sound, that indefinite sound which may be written ' a ' or ' uh ', is used in the definite article ' the ' (except when it precedes a vowel sound) the indefinite article, in unaccented syllables and in such short words as ' but ', ' as ', ' that ', etc., except where they are emphatic. Its use is desirable, as it avoids any suggestion of pedantic speech, but it should not be overdone, and articulation must not be allowed to suffer through its use.

Vowel sounds alone are of no use for the purpose of speech. They have to be combined with consonant sounds, which, in their turn, must be clearly uttered. Again, it is impossible to use consonant sounds alone as a means of communication; we need both the vowel and the consonant sounds. But, unless each sound is perfectly pronounced, speech cannot be really clear.

Many authorities hold that, where a diphthong is followed by ' r ' as in ' hire ', ' pure ' and so on, this is a triphthong. Surely there is danger here that ' pure ' may

be spoken to rhyme with ' ewer '. ' Flower ', ' higher ',
' ewer ' and ' sower ' may be regarded as triphthongs, but
' hire ', ' flour ', ' pure ' and similar sounds, must be
diphthongs followed by ' r '.

TRIPHTHONGAL VOWEL SOUNDS

As their name suggests, there are three vowel sounds in
Triphthongs, for example:

eh-ĭ-a	(the neutral)	as in player
o-oo-a	,,	,,	,, ,, sower
ah-ĭ-a	,,	,,	,, ,, higher
ĭ-oo-a	,,	,,	,, ,, fewer
aw-ĭ-a	,,	,,	,, ,, annoyer
ah-oo-a	,,	,,	,, ,, power

Great care must be taken to avoid making triphthongs
in such words as ' pure ' which is a diphthong, followed by
r; and diphthongs of ' more ', ' war ' and so on, and
pronouncing them as ' maw-er ', and ' waw-er '.

One could quote numerous examples of triphthongal
vowel sounds. They occur, for instance in ' betrayal ',
' aorta ', ' rowan ', ' phial ', ' fuel ', ' Samoyed ', and many
more words.

THE CONSONANT SOUNDS

Consonant sounds are made by the breath alone, or the
voice, *and* a contact, or very close approximation, of two
or more of the organs of speech, i.e. lips, teeth, tongue, hard
and soft palates. Sustained consonant sounds are made
by the passage of breath or voice between organs of speech
which are gently touching, or are very close together, such
as z, sh, v, and so on, or by the mouth passage being
stopped, and the voice passing through the nasal passages,
as in m, n, and ng. Explosives are made by the complete
closing of the vocal passage by the contact of the organs,
followed by their rapid separation, for example, b, t, and k.

There are twenty-four consonant sounds. Of these, fifteen are vocal, or voiced consonants, and nine aspirate, or breath consonants. In most cases there is an aspirate equivalent to a voiced consonant.

Explosive Consonant Sounds

Vocal	*Aspirate*
(1) b as in babe.	(1) p as in peep.
(4) d ,, ,, deed.	(4) t ,, ,, tart.
(6) j ,, ,, judge	(6) ch ,, ,, church.
(5) g ,, ,, gig.	(5) k ,, ,, kick.

Sustained Consonant Sounds

(1) m as in mime.	
(4) n ,, ,, nine.	
(2) v ,, ,, verve.	(2) f as in fluff.
(4) l ,, ,, lull.	
(5) ng ,, ,, singing.	
(6) z ,, ,, buzzes.	(6) s ,, ,, sister.
(6) zh ,, ,, pleasure.	(6) sh ,, ,, sheet.
(5) y ,, ,, you.	
(4) r ,, ,, perish.	
(3) th ,, ,, then.	(3) th ,, ,, thick.
(1) w ,, ,, well.	(1) wh ,, ,, where.

('y', 'w' and 'wh' are now usually classified as semi-vowels. See p. 24 and Appendix.)

The sounds in the foregoing list of consonants are classified thus:

(1) Labials (made by the lips).
(2) Labio-dentals (lip and teeth).
(3) Lingua-dentals (tip of tongue and top front teeth).
(4) Lingua-palatals (tip of tongue and front of hard palate; teeth ridge).
(5) Gutturals (back of tongue and soft palate).
(6) Here the lips, hard palate, tongue and teeth are all brought into action.

There is more than one sound in correctly spoken English for the consonant written r: the trilled r as in 'perish', and the palatal, as in 'war'. Some controversy exists as to the sounding of the final r's, but ideally it is desirable to do so if the purity of the language is to be maintained. Again, there is a fine distinction between such words as 'lord' and 'laud', which makes desirable a recognition of the presence or absence of the consonant r. On the other hand, the introduction of an r sound where none should be, must be carefully avoided. One frequently hears such phrases as 'I have an idearof it', 'Adarand I came', and so on.

It should be noted that for the sounds n and l, the position of the organs is almost identical. The difference in the sound is caused by the fact that in l the resonance is in the mouth, and in n it is more in the nose because in l the tongue is free at the sides, and in n it is pressed against the top side teeth. The most nasal of the consonants are m, n, and ng.

The aspirate h is often included in lists of consonants, but this is incorrect, since it depends for utterance upon neither contact nor approximation of the organs of speech. It is just breath. It is also true that wh, w, and y are not pure consonants. The sounds are made as much by *movement* as by contact or approximation of the organs.

Various combinations of vowels and consonants make the vehicle of our expression of ideas—words.

There are several terms relating to the utterance of words, which are generally used more or less synonymously; but actually each of them has its message and counsel of perfection for the elocution student. 'Articulation' is clear utterance, with special relation to consonant sounds; in fact, 'consonant sound' is a dictionary definition of the word. 'Enunciation', which springs from the Latin *e*, out, and *nunciare*, to tell, means articulate utterance. 'Pronunciation', ('*pro*,' forth; '*nunciare*,' to tell) is 'speech with proper sound and accent'; it refers, not only to consonants, but to every department of speech.

To be properly pronounced, a word must be spoken with correct stress, clear consonants, and well-shaped vowels. All of which brings us so the word ' speech ' itself. This is ' the faculty of uttering articulate sounds ', and we are accustomed to use the word as a synonym for ' diction ', which is ' the expression of ideas by words.' ' Talk ' is familiar speech, or conversation. Our goal, where articulation and pronunciation are concerned, is diction. We are striving to express thoughts and ideas by the spoken word. It is only reasonable to wish to express ourselves as clearly and distinctly as possible. And yet, how few people really do express themselves clearly! How many hours must be wasted in a year, in any business office, through indistinct utterance! What an appalling amount of valuable time is lost while a person addressed asks that a sentence imperfectly heard should be repeated, and while the speaker says the sentence over again. All this would be rectified if people were able, and not too lazy, to enunciate clearly. Articulation is an absolute necessity to the worker, in whatever walk of life. The study of elocution is such a real need, that it will be used and developed more and more, and in the near future will form not only a valuable but an essential part of the education of our boys and girls.

Unfortunately, it is to be feared that elocution, in the minds of many people, means pedantic or ' stagey ' speech. But this is far from the truth. The word ' elocution ' means, literally, a ' speaking out ', for it is derived from two Latin words—*e*, out; and *loqui*, to speak. But obviously there is more in it than merely speaking out. It may be better defined as the ' art of perfect speech '.

Now, let it be emphasized at once, that pedantic speech can never be perfect, because it is so very unnatural. Affectation is a terrible complaint, and the accent assumed by many educated people is infinitely farther removed from perfect speech than a good, honest dialect. That, at any rate, is not ' put on '. As Hamlet has it—' if you mouth it . . . I had as lief the town-crier spoke my lines.'

The speaker must strive to be clear without overdoing articulation. Duplicated consonants here present rather a difficulty. To sound only one tends toward slovenliness; to sound both becomes pedantic. The happy medium is to articulate the first carefully, and then, without breaking the contact of the organs, to carry the sound on with added pressure. For example, take the phrase ' Good-day '. ' Goodday ' is slovenly, ' Good^vday ', over precise. ' Good-*d*ay ' meets the need exactly.

We must look, not only to consonant sounds, but to *every* sound. The impression received by the Scotch girl in *The Fortune of Christina M'Nab*, when first she mixes with English people, is not in the least exaggerated. ' Good-mawning, Lawd Gawge ' they say, and ' I'm going to write to the Staws '. Which of us has not heard English so maltreated?

Ideally, there ought to be a difference in sound between the words ' lord ' and ' laud '; ' paw ', ' pore ', and ' poor '; ' morning ' and ' mourning '? The terminations of ' idea ' and ' hear ' should vary slightly. There should be some distinction between ' wholly ' and ' holy '.

It should be the aim of every one to speak *pure* English, to utter each sound clearly, and to shape every vowel sound correctly, without distortion. Otherwise we shall, in time, lose English, and, in its place, have a nondescript language, devoid of beauty, and without character and individuality.

There are many **Phonetics Terms** now in general use; some of the most usual are:

Affricative	. .	A plosive followed by a fricative.
Alveolar	. .	Made with the tongue-tip.
Fricative	. .	A sustained aspirate consonant sound.
The Lateral	. .	The consonant sound l, where the tongue-tip is against the teeth-ridge and the sides free.
Plosive	. . .	Explosive.
Velar	. . .	Made with the soft palate.

NOTES UPON SOME DEFECTS AND COMMON FAULTS
OF SPEECH

The sound in English which suffers most from speech defect is undoubtedly the sibilant s, and its voiced equivalent z, which can be mispronounced in a variety of ways. The defect is often easily cured, and is simply the result of a wrong adjustment of the organs of speech.

The sibilant is made by raising the tip of the tongue toward the back of the top front teeth, so that it very gently touches, except for a tiny channel in the middle, through which the air flows. The sides of the tongue touch the upper side teeth. The upper and lower front teeth touch, and should be seen between the lips.

Defective s sounds are often caused by a cleft between the front teeth, for which, in adults, there is no cure, except the extraction of these teeth and the wearing of a denture. A child's teeth can generally be regulated by skilful treatment. This also applies when the defect is caused by projecting teeth. In cases where the upper teeth ridge is so formed that perfect regulation is impossible, a slight thickness will always be heard in the articulation of sibilants. An upper or a lower lip which is over long often presents difficulty in sounding s clearly, but, particularly where the upper lip is the cause of the trouble, careful practise under skilled direction will generally right this very quickly.

Those are the most usual organic causes of bad sibilants, with the exception of cleft palate, which is outside the province of this book.

The teacher of speech is perhaps more frequently confronted by students who use their organs of speech wrongly, and either substitute another consonant sound for s or z, or make some particular sound instead. Many children use th for s, that is, they press the tip of the tongue against the top teeth, and can quickly correct the fault if it is pointed out, together with the correct position of the tongue and teeth. Some use an f sound, made with the upper teeth and lower lip, which can be righted in the same way as the th sound. Placing the tongue too far back on the teeth ridge, and deepening the channel through which the air passes, causes a sh sound for s. A less common defect, and one which is not so easy to treat, is caused by approximating the back of the tongue and the soft palate, thus making what is called by phoneticians, voiceless ng. The student, in such cases, must be taught to raise the soft palate, as well as to place the tongue in the correct position. Unless there is some defect which prevents the soft palate from rising, it doubtless goes up for other sounds, and its position then should be noted by the student, particularly in open vowels, like ah. Voiceless l is made by placing the tongue in the same position as for the consonant l, and aspirating.

' Dark ' l is made when the tongue-tip is placed too far back on the hard palate.

If the tongue tip is placed too far forward when saying t, the result will be a sibilant sound resembling ' ts '.

Exercises to help sufferers from these defects can always be devised by a teacher, once the trouble is diagnosed and explained to the student.

There are many other defects and faults of speech which may be corrected by careful study, such as using f for th, n or nk for ng, a voiceless ng for th, and so on. They do not arise from any defect in the speaking apparatus, but quite frequently from carelessness, or ignorance.

All defects and difficulties may be cured far more readily so soon as a student really understands his fault, and knows at what position of the organs he is aiming.

Now to turn to general faults as distinct from those connected with particular sounds.

The very common fault of **Inaudibility** at the ends of sentences is generally caused by dropping the voice through lack of breath. Many inexperienced speakers attempt longer phrases than they can manage, and so cannot keep up the tone. Until they have gained greater breath control, they should break up their sentences into shorter phrases. Also, it is necessary for all speakers to study the rules of inflection and pitch, and to learn not to drop the voice at the end of a sentence.

A fairly common fault is the **Rebound**—adding a neutral vowel sound after a final consonant, thus, ' That's good-uh '. This is partly a matter of lack of breath control, and is often caused, to some extent, by nervousness. If the student is told of this fault, and studies its correction, together with breath control exercises, the defect soon disappears.

Nasal Tone is caused by the improper functioning of the soft palate, which should be raised toward the back of the pharynx for all sounds except the nasal consonants. The soft palate descends for the guttural consonants, and for those with nasal resonance—ng, n and m in particular. Frequently after making these sounds, the soft palate is too slow in assuming a position in which it leaves free the passage into the mouth, and nasal tone results. If this is pointed out, and the student watches the movement of the soft palate in a mirror, the fault is not difficult to remedy. Nasal tone must not be confused with nasal resonance, or with the fault known as ' talking through the nose '. Nasal resonance is the pleasant ringing tone which results from the proper use of the nasal cavities in voice-production. The fault of ' talking through the nose ' is, as a matter of fact, quite wrongly so called. It would be more accurate to describe it as talking *without* the nose, which can be demonstrated by closing the nostrils during loud phonation, when exactly this tone will result.

The complete stoppage of the nasal passages encountered in bad cases of adenoids is, of course, quite in a different category. Here, the resonance cavities of the nose are blocked by the growth, and no nasal resonance can be obtained. The result is deadness of tone, and an inability to pronounce any of the nasal consonants; n, in these cases, becomes l. The sufferer is, of course, unable to breathe through the nose. After an operation for adenoids it is necessary to teach a patient to use the nasal cavities by breathing exercises, humming, singing, etc. Cases of slight adenoids may often be cured, if taken in good time, by such exercises, particularly singing exercises on n and ng sounds.

Monotony in speech generally arises from one of several causes; either too little inflection is used, in fact the words are almost intoned; or the same inflection is repeated over and over again; or else the pitch is not varied sufficiently— in other words, there is no modulation. People who speak monotonously generally do so because they have not learned to listen to themselves, and their ear is not developed. If they will listen to, and try to imitate, accomplished speakers, they will, with practice, learn modulation.

On the other hand, it is most irritating to listen to over-inflective speech. It gives an effect of insincerity and artificiality. The best remedy is, again, for the speaker to learn to listen to himself, and also to practise speaking in a monotone, when the very contrast will bring home to him the fault of over-inflection, and help him to check it.

The **Hiatus**—the concurrence of vowel sounds in a word or at the end of one word and the beginning of the next—often presents great difficulty. Speakers are inclined to introduce a consonant sound where none should be, with disastrous effect. One hears, ' It is thawring '. ' I had no widearof it ', 'Any yother time ', and so on. This is a fault most difficult to overcome, and the student's struggles for mastery often result in his producing, instead, sounds preceded by a **Glottal Stop.**

This, as its name implies, is a brief closing and opening of the glottis.[1] It is often used by those who are striving to speak emphatically, or to articulate with great precision. The sound, written in the phonetic alphabet ' ? ', is also heard very frequently in Cockney and North-Country dialects, instead of t. For instance, we hear ' Pu ? the ke ?le on ' for ' Put the kettle on '. As these dialects include t sounds initially in other words, treatment is not difficult.

Those who introduce the sound at the beginning of words commencing with vowel sounds, and where the

[1] See Appendix.

hiatus occurs in a word, should practise relaxation and singing sustained vowel sounds, first preceded by m, then alone, thus: moo, maw, mah, moh, etc., moo, oo, maw, aw, etc., first without, and then with, a breath between the sounds. As soon as the glottal stop makes itself heard, the m sound should be introduced again.

Another helpful exercise is for the student to speak verse with the words all joined together, with m preceding lines which commence with a vowel. As soon as he becomes used to the sensation of the flow of voice through the constantly open glottis during speech, the defect will disappear.

Although quite a common defect, and in itself not serious, the introduction of the glottal stop is a fault which needs to be checked, because of the injurious effect on the larynx of the continual closing and re-opening of the glottis.

CHAPTER IV

THE QUICKSILVER, OR THE POWER OF REFLEC-
TION: OUR MEANS OF EXPRESSION (I)

' . . . the purpose of playing, whose end . . . was, and is, to hold, as
't were, the mirror up to nature '.

NOW THAT WE have examined the structural parts of our
mirror, and have seen how we may use and preserve them,
let us turn to the mirror's power of reflection—our various
means of expression.

First, then, what is the function of words? What are
we trying to achieve by means of words, whether spoken
or written? We are trying to express ideas. Every
word we speak is the outward expression of a thought
within the mind.

The reciter is not, as a rule, expressing his own ideas,
but he is striving to suggest to his audience the visions
which the written thought of another has conjured up in
his mind. First of all, it is necessary for him to perform
two distinct mental exercises. He must read, think upon,
and memorize the poem before him, and so gain his own
perception of the picture which the author has painted.
Then he must evolve the means by which he may paint
again, through his mirror, the picture which the poet first
saw. He must be as sure as in him lies that he is not
distorting the picture, throwing into it high lights which
were not in the original, changing its aspect, destroying
its harmony. He must decide just how far his own
personality may be used to colour his reproduction, and to
what extent he must suppress and subjugate the personal
touch. To make his reproduction perfect, he uses every
means of expression in his power, and here it is that he
will begin to reap the benefit of his work.

His study of voice-production and articulation will bring
its reward, his mirror will be bright and clear. It will
enable him to throw light and shade into his work, to
paint his picture with a delicate and unerring touch.

VOCAL EXPRESSION

EMPHASIS AND PAUSE

One of the simplest means of expression we use, which
comes quite naturally to every one, is **Emphasis**—that
stress or accent which we lay upon words to which we wish
to attach special importance. It is possible to convey a
totally different meaning by speaking the same words with
varied emphasis. For instance, supposing a customer in a
shop says to an assistant: ' I asked for a *blue* dress.' This
conveys that she had been shown a dress, but of the wrong
colour. ' I asked for a blue *dress* ' shows that the colour
was right, but the garment wrong; she had been shown a
coat or a suit. ' *I* asked for a blue dress ' indicates
that the speaker, out of several people, was the one to
make the request. We can change the meaning, in every
case, by transferring the emphasis.

Another way in which we can emphasize is by inflection.
If, instead of stress being laid upon it, a word is spoken
with a compound inflection, it is made to stand out very
distinctly, and that without the voice being raised in the
least. This will be referred to again in the notes on
inflections.

There is still another, and an even more telling manner
in which words and phrases may be made to stand out
from their context, and that is by making effective use of
Pause.

We make constant use of three distinct cessations of the
voice in elocution. There is **Grammatical Pause,** which
divides our matter coherently into sentences, and by which
we indicate the presence of punctuation marks. We take
advantage of these pauses, as a rule, for the purpose of
breathing.

Dramatic pause, or **pause for effect,** is the slight holding up of the voice which should occur at the end of each line of verse. This will be mentioned later, when the subject of speaking verse is discussed.[1]

The third is **Rhetorical Pause,** which is used to give particular weight to words where stress or inflection is unsuitable or not sufficiently strong to meet the case. Rhetorical pause is a tremendously powerful means of expression which is, unfortunately, far too often neglected. As an example, consider the last words of the dying Queen Katharine in *Henry VIII*: ' I can no more '. Emphasis here would be quite out of place, and, in any case, it would be beyond the Queen's failing strength. So, speak the words with an appreciable pause, thus: ' I can ^v no more '. Note the effect which is gained; a tremendous effect of a woman in the extremity of sorrow and weariness.

So many speakers, beginners in particular, are afraid to pause, because it seems to them that they are dragging. When they stop speaking, even for a second or two, the resulting silence appals them, and seems to last for an unconscionable time. Besides, most of us, when we first begin to raise our voices in public, are anxious to say what we have to say, and get it over. Consequently, we speak as quickly as possible, and our pauses—often so carefully rehearsed—go by the board, with unfortunate results. Now, here is a slogan for any one who is learning to speak in public, whether it be as a reciter, a preacher, an actor, or a public speaker; *Mind Your Pauses*. Remember that the pause which seems so long to you really lasts for only a few seconds. **Nonetheless you** must pause to allow your audience time to realize what you are saying— every phrase must be given a chance to sink in. If you speak quickly and without quite appreciable breaks, the torrent of your words will sweep over your hearers, leaving them no wiser than they were before. That does not necessarily mean that you were inaudible. Quite possibly

[1] See p. 69.

your audience could *hear* every word.   Only, if you do not
pause, they will not have time to absorb what they hear.

When you have the opportunity, listen to great speakers.
Notice how effectively they use the pause, and how greatly
their speech gains power and vividness thereby.   One of
our famous actors,—I think, Sir Herbert Tree,—was even
said to be ' eloquent in his pauses '.   Any one, then, who
aspires to become an accomplished speaker, has to learn
to make the fullest use of pause.

Now, as to pause with regard to phrasing, a phrase
being the group of words spoken in a breath.   Beginners
generally tend to commit one or other of two faults in
this direction: either they attempt too much in a phrase,
or they take breath so frequently that they break the
continuity of the sentence.   Sometimes, indeed, it is
difficult to induce small children to refrain from breathing
in the middle of a word!

At a rehearsal of the Croydon Triennial Musical Festival,
Sir Henry J. Wood gave this piece of advice to the Chorus,
which was losing tone through attempting to sing, in a
breath, more than was convenient or comfortable: ' When
you are preparing to sing in public, make sure that you are
able to sing, in practice, each of your phrases twice over
in one breath.   Then you will be quite sure of yourself,
and nervousness will not make you breathless.'

That is most excellent advice both for singers and for
speakers who attempt phrases which are over-long.   Those
who go to the other extreme need to study breath-control
with particular care, and practise speaking passages which
have been marked for phrasing.

INFLECTION

Probably we have all had experience, at one time or
another, of the truth of the saying, that it is not what we
say that counts, but how we say it.   How we say things
depends to a great extent upon **Inflection,** the rise and fall

of the voice, by which we may put the most delicate shades of meaning into the words we speak. The word springs from the same Latin root (*flexus*, a bending) as the word ' flexible '. Have we not all found that a letter, written with the kindest of thoughts and the best of intentions, may give an entirely wrong impression to its recipient? Simply because it was written, so to speak, in one tone of voice, and read in another. If the sender of the letter had spoken the words instead of writing them, all would have been well. Inflection would have made his intention clear, even though the words were ill-chosen.

The argument is sometimes heard that the study of rules of inflection tends to make speech dull and stilted. But why should it? No one would ever dream of saying that the practice of degrees of touch, when learning to play the piano, robs the subsequent performance of life and spontaneity. Quite the reverse, in fact. Everybody knows that many hours of practice are necessary before one can play the piano or the violin in public. Why should not the same rule apply with equal force to so delicate and complicated an instrument as the human speaking apparatus?

Rules of inflection have not been invented and applied to studied speech. Experience has proved that we use certain inflections in certain cases when we are speaking naturally. The rules have merely resulted from the observations of experts, who have noted what inflections we use to express all kinds of ideas and emotions, and tabulated them. The necessity for the rules arises from our inability to register our natural inflections and apply them to our studied speech. Unless a speaker has some knowledge of these laws, he is, indeed, apt to become very monotonous. Nearly every public speaker is deserted, when he is nervous, by the natural rise and fall of his voice, and, unless he has a good foundation of technical knowledge to support him will probably repeat the same inflection (generally a downward one) *ad lib.*, and so become uninteresting in the extreme.

Test the rules which are given below, when you are speaking naturally. You will find that they come quite freely to you, without effort or any unnatural feeling.

Upward Inflections are used in the following cases:

1. Entreaties, pleas, and requests:

   ' Oh, spare him.'   ' Let him in.'   ' Pass the salt.'

2. Incomplete statements:

   ' . . . and our boyhood ceased—well, when ? '

   > Robert Louis Stevenson, *Virginibus Puerisque*.

   ' Scrooge was his sole executor, his sole adminis-trator, his sole assign, his sole residuary legatee, his sole friend, his sole mourner.'

   > Dickens, *A Christmas Carol*.

   (Here the statement might be completed—making perfect sense—at any comma. ' Scrooge was his sole executor ' is a good and finished sentence, but in this case the statement is incomplete. It is not finished until the phrase ' his sole mourner ' is reached. The only way in which the speaker is able to indicate this, is by giving each phrase an upward inflection until the statement is completed when this, in its turn, is indicated by a downward inflection.)

3. Negative clauses (except when they are strongly emphatic):

   ' Presume not on thy heart when mine is slain;

   Thou gavest me thine, not to give back again.'

   > Shakespeare, *Sonnet XXII*.

4. Parentheses (which are spoken more quickly than the context, and in a lower pitch):

' But let my words, *the words of one so small,*

Who, knowing nothing, knows but to obey,

And if I do not there is penance given,

Comfort your sorrows.'

Tennyson, *Guinevere.*

5. Qualifying phrases:

' " My fault " she wept, " my fault! and yet not mine;

Yet mine in part." '

Tennyson, *The Princess.*

6. Questions which can be answered by yes or no:

' Cannot thy master sleep these tedious nights? '
Shakespeare, *Richard III.*

7. Retorted questions:

' Mother: " Why were you crying just now? "

' Girl: " Why was I crying? " '
Gilbert Cannan, *Everbody's Husband.*

(Notice that this rule holds, although the question commences with an interrogative, and in the first place, takes a downward inflection.)

8. The first member of alternative questions:

' Have I the pleasure of addressing Mr. Scrooge or Mr. Marley? '

Dickens, *A Christmas Carol.*

9. Climax: (To give effect to climax the phrases preceding it should take rising inflections.)

> ' Look to 't, think on't, I do not use to jest,
> Thursday is near; lay hand on heart, advise:
> An you be mine, I'll give you to my friend;
> An you be not, hang, beg, starve, die in the
> streets,
> For, by my soul, I'll ne'er acknowledge thee,
> Nor what is mine shall never do thee good:
> Trust to't, bethink you; I'll not be forsworn.'
>> Shakespeare, *Romeo and Juliet.*

(Nearly all these phrases take upward inflections,
working up to ' I'll not be forsworn ' and the
exit of Capulet.)

Downward Inflections are used for:

1. Complete statements, finality:

> ' For men may come and men may go
> But I go on for ever.'
>> Tennyson, *The Brook.*

2. Commands:

> ' Give me some music: '
>> Shakespeare, *Antony and Cleopatra.*

3. Exclamations:

> ' What triumph! Hark—what pain! '
>> Matthew Arnold, *Philomela.*

4. The second member of alternative questions:

> ' Have I the pleasure of addressing Mr. Scrooge
> or Mr. Marley? '
>> Dickens, *A Christmas Carol.*

5. Questions commencing with or consisting of an interrogative, i.e. how? where? which? when? who? etc.

' How fares my noble lord? '

When?   Whither?

6. Strongly emphatic negative sentences:

' Pardon me, you are not engaged to any one.'
Oscar Wilde, *The Importance of Being Ernest.*

' No, faith, I'll not stay a jot longer.'
Shakespeare, *Twelfth Night.*

Compound Inflections are used to express:

1. Incredulity:

' What!   Not Lily Pierce? Lord, he didn't marry her? '

Clemance Dane, *Mariners.*

2. Doubt, uncertainty:

' If we should fail? '

Shakespeare, *Macbeth.*

3. Sarcasm, Irony:

' Ay, marry, sir, now looks he like a king.'
Shakespeare, *Henry VI*, The Mockery of York by Queen Margaret.

4. Where the meaning is greater than is expressed by the words:
' My lord's almost so far transported that
He'll think anon it lives '
Shakespeare, *The Winter's Tale.*

5. The second member of an antithesis:

> ' . . . its feigned assent which might so likely cloak an obstinate dissent.'
>
> Anthony Hope.

> ' I must be gone and live, or stay and die.'
>
> Shakespeare, *Romeo and Juliet.*

6. Implied antithesis:

> ' *Murderer.* We are men, my liege.
>
> *Macbeth.* Ay, in the catalogue ye go for men.'
>
> Shakespeare, *Macbeth.*

Emphasis may be given by the use of a compound inflection:

> ' To sleep; perchance to dream; ay, there's the rub.'
>
> Shakespeare, *Hamlet.*

Antitheses, as a rule, take a generally upward inflection on one member, and a downward on the other.

Repeated questions, where we ask a question again of ourselves or of another, take the same inflection as the original question, but generally with greater emphasis.

Inversions, where the words are not in their usual order, take an upward inflection, except when they are used for the purpose of emphasis:

> ' For they said, " As a lady should lie, lies she! " '
>
> Sir Edwin Arnold, *He and She.*

> ' Go he must.'

It must always be remembered that artistic effect must prove an exception to all rules of inflection. Thus, although the sentences are incomplete, falling inflections would be used to give an effect of sorrow or gloom:

> ' Say! You've struck a heap of trouble—
>
> Bust in business, lost your wife; '
>
> Robert Service, *Comfort.*

MODULATION

' . . . in the very torrent, tempest and . . . whirlwind of passion, you must acquire and beget a temperance that may give it smoothness.'

Modulation, in music, means a change of key; a shifting of the tonality of a piece. In speech, it means the continual play upon inflections, the ever-changing rise and fall of the voice.

It means, too, the use of the voice according to subject matter, and also according to the size and acoustic properties of the room in which one is speaking. We should not use the same tone, power and quality, if we recited ' The Hound of Heaven ' in the Albert Hall, as if we did ' There are Fairies at the Bottom of Our Garden ' in some one's drawing-room. We must modulate our voices to suit the conditions.

Modulation, then, includes pitch; rate, or pace; and intensity. Let us examine these individually.

Pitch. We speak, as we sing, on the notes of a scale, the voice being inflected over groups of several notes, which are in the upper, middle, and lower pitch, corresponding to the registers of the singing voice. We pass continually from one group of notes to another. The range of the speaking voice is not so great as that of the singing voice, and we speak, in ordinary conversation, over about five notes in the middle of our full range. That is called the Middle Pitch. When we express excitement and kindred emotions, and when we are talking about fairies, whispering breezes, and so on, we lift our voices, using the Upper Pitch. For heavy work, and to convey sorrow, depression, gloom, we use the Lower Pitch.

The advice one so often hears addressed to speakers to ' speak up ' is, in many cases—as Mr. Alexander Watson points out in his splendid book *Speak Out*—quite a mistake. To speak *up* would be merely to raise the pitch. What the speakers in question are required to do is to make themselves more audible, to speak *out*, which is a matter of articulation and projection rather than of pitch.

Pace, or speed. As a rule it is easy to decide whether a piece should be taken quickly or slowly. The subject matter settles that. But speakers generally are inclined not to use enough variety, and to speak at too unvarying a pace throughout, say, a part in a play, or a poem. It is a subject which requires careful thought, for skilfully varied speed of delivery may make all the difference between a good performance and a perfect one.

Here, a word of advice to the novice. When you make your first public appearance, the chances are that nervousness will cause one idea to take possession of your mind: to get it over as quickly as possible, no matter how. Now make up your mind firmly on this point: you will not be hurried. You have practised what you have to say, at a certain pace, and at that pace you will deliver it. It must on no account be allowed to run away with you. Get that idea firmly into your head; then no nervous fancies about ' getting it over quickly ' will stand a chance, and your performance will be just as it should be. It will help you, too, to bear in mind the fact that your words are intended to reach, not only the highly intelligent people in the front of the hall, but also those in the farthest corner, among whom may be some whose hearing is not of the best, and whose minds move slowly. Imagine an old gentleman, deaf, and seated in the back row. Project your speech *to him*. Do not shout, but articulate very distinctly, and do not speak too fast. Take time to make clearly every consonant sound—initial, internal and final— and to shape every vowel sound. And remember that, until your articulation is extremely good, it is unwise to attempt anything which requires rapid speech.

Power, or **Intensity.** This is that vibrant quality which conveys emotional excitement and dramatic feeling. It does not depend upon loudness or upon raised pitch, in fact, just the reverse. Words spoken in a whisper, with feeling and conviction, may be far more intense than the same words delivered with big vocal tone. Intensity depends mainly upon the feeling behind it—in other words, upon the imagination of the reciter, and its effect is increased by his bearing, his facial expression, and the clearness of his enunciation.

Projection. It is an undoubted fact that something more than a strong, clear voice and good enunciation is needed if a speaker is to make himself audible in every part of a large room or hall—or one that is poor acoustically. The necessary quality is Projection. The speaker must *consciously* direct his speech to the furthest corner of the building. If he fails to do this, his voice may be clearly audible, but not his words; not his message.

It is for this reason that many authorities hold that a reader should not keep his eyes on the book, but look up whenever possible, so that he establishes and keeps contact with the audience. It is very certain that, with an audience of young children, one does not hold their attention unless one looks at them to maintain communication.

Restraint. Intensity is, to a great extent, dependent upon restraint. Unless the expression of passions and emotions is held in check, a torrent of words will pour forth, gesture and movement will get almost out of control, and intensity will be lost. There are times, of course, when visible restraint has to be shed, and the effect of uncontrolled emotion given, but the actor and reciter must never, for an instant, lose his grip upon himself.

CHAPTER V

OUR MEANS OF EXPRESSION (II): EXPRESSION OTHER THAN VOCAL

FACIAL EXPRESSION

' to show virtue her own feature, scorn her own image,'

IF WE ARE willing to accept the view that, to be beautiful, speech must be natural, we should readily admit that we are bound to reflect, in facial expression, the thought which we are striving to express.

Most of us naturally express our thoughts in our faces (sometimes rather too much, with embarrassing consequences!), and this natural gift of expression is used and cultivated by the reciter. Whatever question there may be with regard to the use of facial expression when reciting lyrics, there can be none where dramatic and character work is concerned. The student has to learn to express emotion in his face as well as in his voice.

Now, it is very often the case that, so soon as some one who has, naturally, quite an expressive countenance, begins to speak or recite studied words, nervous self-consciousness removes all trace of expression, and leaves the face utterly blank and mask-like. Such people find it quite impossible to believe that they are presenting expressionless countenances. Their sensations become so exaggerated that a faint wrinkle between the brows feels like a dark scowl, and an almost imperceptible smile, like a broad grin. If they catch sight of themselves in the glass, they are amazed to find that they are not ' registering emotion ' at all!

When able to register any emotion at will, the student should practise reciting, or he will find that, in thinking about the words, he forgets his expression and his

45

face becomes blank again. This 'blankness' is not very difficult to overcome — practice and care will soon put it right.

GESTURE

' Nor do not saw the air too much with your hand, . . . but use all gently; '

It is a true saying that there are exceptions to every rule, but it is, perhaps, more true of the rules for the use of gesture than of most things, so the rules given below, are merely suggestions which may prove helpful to those practising gesture.

The speaker, and sometimes the actor, is rather apt to forget that gesture is a means to an end, not an end in itself. What is that end? Why do we use gesture at all?

Diction, as we have seen already, is the expression of ideas by words. It is natural to us, when we speak, to help that expression, by the use of our hands, and by the posture of our bodies. It is these movements, perfectly natural and unstudied as they are, which form the basis of the rules of gesture which have been drawn up for the guidance of students of elocution and dramatic art.

It is most unusual for any one to use, in ordinary conversation, a gesture which is inexpressive and stiff. It is with action, just as it is with facial expression: self-consciousness causes us to become awkward, and so we make movements which are wrong, not because they fail to conform to some rigid standard, but because they are stiff, unnatural and ineffective. Bad gesture defeats its own end. Its very wrongness draws attention to it, and, instead of making a picture clearer, it distracts the minds of the audience from what is said, and focuses them upon the movement which is made.

Relaxation of the muscles of the whole body is most important. Any tension will at once cause ' wooden-doll ' movements, and it has already been pointed out how needful is relaxation because of its beneficial effect upon the voice. There are moments, of course, when the required intensity of the situation can be obtained only by tenseness of the body. But this is not to say that a tense and rigid bearing is a good habit for the student to form. He should be capable of speaking any lines with perfect relaxation, reserving his powers for the time when they are truly needed.

(A few exercises follow at the end of the Chapter.)

1. Never overload speech with gesture.
2. All gestures should move on curves from the centre of the body. But remember that the picture presented when a gesture is complete is of more importance than the movement itself.
3. The picture should be held for a few seconds.
4. A gesture should be followed with the eyes.
5. A gesture should precede or accompany the most important word in a sentence.
6. The bigger the subject, the bigger the gesture. Slight conversational movements may come from the wrist, but exultation, fury,—all the great emotions—need the full sweep of the arm.
7. If possible, avoid crossing the body with the arm. Use the arm and leg farthest from the audience. When kneeling on one knee, let it be the one nearest the audience.
8. Gestures accompanying requests, offers, and so on, are generally made with the hand palm upward; of refusal, negation, etc., with the palm downward.

STANCE

It has already been hinted that the pose of the body is a matter which requires the careful attention of the speaker and reciter. There are two things which he must learn to do: stand straight, and stand still.

So many people allow themselves to get into the habit of standing with one foot in front of the other, and the weight thrown on to the *backward* one. This is a very bad position. In the first place, it does not allow of the weight of the body being evenly distributed among the muscles designed to bear it. In the second place, it looks sloppy and ungainly. And in the third place, much freedom of movement is lost by standing in this way. One is not ready to make the swift changes of position which so often are necessary.

The ideal position is with the feet slightly apart, the weight being born equally by both, and tending forward on to the ball of the foot. If, as is sometimes the case, this feels unnatural, then one foot may be a little before the other, with the weight placed upon the *forward* foot. Thus, you will stand straight.

It is well to give effect to change of subject when speaking, by a change of position. This may be done by transferring the weight from one foot to the other, being careful to keep forward the foot which is to receive your weight, unless, of course, there is some reason to the contrary.

Gesture is frequently accompanied by a definite change in the balance of the body. Threatening movements, and those expressive of entreaty, of protectiveness and the like, take forward balance, when a step is taken and the weight thrown well forward. Gestures expressing scorn, cowardice, surprise, and so on, take backward balance.

It is not difficult to determine what position is required for any given moment. If you are expressing some emotion which will take you toward the subject, forward balance is required. If you would naturally draw back or recoil, then backward balance will meet the need.

To turn to the second point: standing still. By this it is not meant that a speaker should stand as though glued to the floor. Far from it—freedom of movement is essential. But to move freely does not mean to fidget. Those who make little fussy, unnecessary movements, who sway from one foot to the other (this is a special temptation when reciting verse), and who shuffle their feet, must make a really determined effort to break themselves of these habits. Otherwise they will never do really good work. They must learn to move only when occasion requires.

Remember always the importance of walking onto and off a platform, and entering and leaving a room with dignity and composure.

RELAXATION EXERCISES

1. Sit or lie on your back in a comfortable position. Realize that the chair or bed is holding you: you make no effort. Take a deep breath as you stiffen every muscle, beginning at your toes, up to your legs, thighs, body, to the shoulders; down to the finger-tips, up to the top of the head. Hold for a moment. As you breathe out on a loud sigh— RELAX.

2. In the same order, tense and relax each group of muscles separately, breathing in and out with each movement.

3. Let your head roll onto your left shoulder, back, onto the right shoulder, down. Do this twice more, then reverse direction, and repeat thrice.

Never hold your breath when practising these exercises.

PART II

POLISHING AND USING THE MIRROR

CHAPTER VI

SPEAKING AND RECITING IN PUBLIC

'With this special observance, that you o'erstep not the modesty of nature:'

WE HAVE MADE our mirror. We have examined our materials, and have seen, so far as we can, how Nature intends us to use them. We have worked and practised until our mirror is bright and ready for use.

Dame Nature's moods are many and varied, and we must learn to hold the mirror up to her in every one of them. The manner of speech which will reflect her in one humour will certainly not reflect her in another. Perfect speech for the part of Lady Macbeth would be far from perfect for Titania, or for Mistress Quickly. And so we must learn to use our mirror through the media of verse and of prose, of reading aloud, of character study, dramatic work and lyrical poetry. Such a wealth of beauty and interest for us to explore! We soon shall find that it will not do for us to attempt to reflect only one of Nature's aspects, that were too small and narrow an ambition. Even though we cannot all excel in every direction, we must work on the broadest lines possible. We must strive to broaden our minds, to seek Beauty in every form of Art, not only in our particular form.

Certain rules apply equally to the reciter and the speaker:

You must gain

> Command of Subject
> Command of Self
> Command of Audience.

Achieve the first two and the last will follow. Even if you feel very nervous, this will not be obvious if you *know* your words or your subject; stand straight; stand still; use your technique to the full, and your audience will be with you.

When we are giving a public recital, there is a number of particulars which we like to possess when preparing the programme. First of all, we require a few details with regard to the hall or room. How large is it? Has it a platform? Is it good for sound, and easy to speak in? Are there curtains, and any facilities for little properties we may want, and furniture—a table, chairs, and so on? It is well for us to know how much time is allotted to us. Then, the audience. A few particulars on this score are very necessary. The same programme most certainly will not suit every one.

If you are to give an evening's recital, either alone or with another artist, work out the programme very carefully with regard to length. Time each item, and then allow at least one minute to each item for taking your position, leaving the platform, and applause. Never continue after the advertised time of ending, unless your audience makes very clear its desire that you should do so. People begin to look at watches, put on coats, whisper, and fidget generally if a recital continues for long after the time limit. However well you have held their attention, and however interested, as a whole, your audience may be, it is better to send them away wanting more, than feeling that they have had enough. Besides, there are always people who have ordered a car, or arranged to catch a train, according to the time advertised for the recital to end, and they will create a disturbance as they go out.

Vary the programme as much as possible, and keep humorous items until the latter part. Once you have made people laugh, really heartily, it is not easy to get them to settle down to listen with pleasure to heavy or to lyrical pieces.

It is a good plan to include a couple of groups of songs, or solos by an instrumentalist, in a programme of this kind. It greatly eases the strain on the recitalist, rests both his voice and his mind. It gives the audience a complete change. An excellent arrangement for all concerned.

There can be no rule laid down for the memorizing of lines. It is a point which every one must decide for himself by experience. Some people walk about as they learn, some lie or sit as restfully as possible, others write out the words, which is a great help in learning to many people. Others, again, can memorize lines only by speaking them aloud over and over again. One thing alone is certain, and applies in all cases: the more one learns, the more one can. People who are continually taking part in plays, or reciting in public, are nearly always quick studies. Those with notoriously bad memories should try learning a few lines of verse each day, increasing the number with growing facility.

Generally speaking, the following is a sound method of procedure when preparing selections for presentation in public:

Read the piece through to gain an idea of its meaning and suitability — not forgetting your own ability of performance. Read it again more carefully, and with regard to punctuation, phrasing and inflection. (It is always desirable to experiment with inflections before actually learning and practising a piece, for wrongly practised inflections are often very difficult to correct). Then learn it, experimenting with gesture and facial expression, and deciding how best you can make your performance effective in this way. Throughout, say it as often as possible *aloud*.

It is very important that you should practise aloud, because, however well a piece may be known, the unaccustomed sound of one's own voice, added to the nervousness caused by public appearance, will often induce acute 'stage-fright'. It is a disconcerting discovery that one's voice sounds so different from what one expects, when it is lifted up in public. Practise aloud; if possible use a tape-recorder. Get used to the sound of your own voice speaking those particular words. Then the certainty that the words are perfectly known, and can be spoken with the facility that only such practice can give, will help you to gain complete coolness and self-confidence.

CHAPTER VII

VERSE

WHAT IS VERSE? Most people, faced with that question, answer that verse is poetry. So it often is, but not always. Poetry takes other forms than verse. A great deal of prose is most perfect poetry—one could scarcely find anything more truly poetical than certain passages of the Bible. Musically, we have tone-poems, symphonic poems, and so on. A poem is better defined as the beautiful expression of a thought. Verse which fulfils this ideal is poetry. Otherwise, it is merely verse—or perhaps doggerel. Neither does verse depend in any way upon rhyme; if it did, there could be no blank, and no unrhymed verse. No, verse is distinct from prose, in that it has Rhythm.[1]

Response to the appeal of rhythm is natural to each of us; and small wonder, for rhythm is all around us and within us. Throughout Nature—in the swing of the tides, the phases of the moon, the movement of our limbs as we walk, the very beating of our hearts—everywhere, is rhythm. One of the most primitive of musical instruments is the drum, and to-day who can resist its throb, or refrain from falling into step with marching men? Give a child the lid of a biscuit tin and a spoon. He will be supremely happy making a noise, and it will be a rhythmic noise. There lies the appeal of modern Jazz and ' Beat ', not in the music itself, but in the lilt of it. So it is not surprising that the sound of rhythmic words has a deep and potent appeal. Children will sit quietly and listen while verse is read to them, where prose will bore them stiff.

The rhythm is produced in verse, just as it is in music, by accent. Every word in English of more than one syllable (excepting only two, ' Amen ' and ' Farewell '),

[1] From Greek and Latin words meaning ' flow ', ' form ', ' shape '.

has at least one of its syllables stressed to a greater or lesser degree. Words of more than two syllables have often two stresses, one stronger than the other. 'Corridor', for instance, has a marked stress upon the first syllable and a lighter one upon the third. 'Honeysuckle' is stressed strongly on the first, and lightly on the third syllable. Rhythm is the result of the regular recurrence of stressed, among unstressed syllables. Words of one syllable may be used as either light or heavy, at the discretion of the poet. The rhythmic pattern of verse, that is, the collection of corresponding groups of syllables rhythmically arranged, is called Metre.

RHYTHM AND METRE

Let us take a simple illustration of rhythm and metre. Imagine that we have a box of coloured beads, some blue, representing light (unstressed) syllables; some red, representing heavy (stressed) syllables. We arrange our beads in a long line, two blue and one red, one red and two blue, or blue and red alternately, in a definite pattern. Perhaps, here and there, for a change, we make some little irregularity in the pattern to break the monotony, and place two red beads together, or something of that kind. There is our illustration of rhythm.

Now for metre. We decide to thread our beads, so we divide them into sets of so many groups of our red and blue pattern. Then, having threaded them up, we arrange our strings so that they correspond: strings of four groups alternating with strings of three; pairs of strings of the same length, and so on, and collect them into sets which are similar to one another. Which is just what a poet does, using syllables instead of beads. The modern 'free verse' is bound by no conventions—it has neither rhyme nor metre. We also find a great deal of verse which is, metrically, extremely irregular.

Prose has no pattern. Stressed and unstressed syllables are irregularly arranged.

Rhyme, which is so important a part of English verse, is the repetition, at regular intervals, of words with similar terminating, but different initial, sounds. Rhymes may be single, with the rhyme in only one syllable, as ' snow ' and ' go '; double, where two syllables rhyme, as ' tellers ' and ' sellers '; or triple, where the rhyme is in three syllables (of which W. S. Gilbert was so fond) such as ' uniform ' and ' cuneiform '. As a rule, rhyme falls at the ends of lines, but sometimes it is found in the middle as well:

' There is heard a hymn when the panes are dim,
  And never before or again;
  When the nights are strong with a darkness long
  And the dark is alive with rain.'

G. K. Chesterton, A Child of the Snows.

There is very great variety possible in the arrangement of rhyming lines. They may run in couplets, but it is more usual to find alternate lines rhyming, or the second and fourth lines of a verse only. Some poets favour matching their first and fourth lines, with a couplet between, *a b b a*; some carry their rhyming pattern throughout the verses of a poem, the same rhyme recurring in each verse. These are but a few of the most usual of rhyme-patterns, which have infinite possibilities.

Eye-rhyme—This is the use, as rhymes, of words similar in spelling, but not in sound:
' O come with me and be my love
  And we will all the pleasures prove.'

Marlowe, The Passionate Shepherd.

Blank Verse—Although so much English verse is rhymed, verse which has no rhyme is by no means uncommon. Blank verse is unrhymed verse of a particular

metre: iambic pentameters—ten syllables, short-long
alternately, in each line. The plays of Shakespeare are
written almost entirely in this form; Milton and Tennyson
also used it extensively.

As well as metre and rhyme, the poet uses various
means to make his verse effective. It is most necessary
for the reciter to have some knowledge of these embel-
lishments, or it will not be possible for him to give them
their true value. Those most usual in English verse are:

1. **Alliteration**—The use of the same initial sound in
   words more or less in juxtaposition:

   ' O marvellously modest maiden, you! '
                          Tennyson, *The Princess.*

2. **Assonance,** or **Vowel-Rhyme.** This imperfect
   form of rhyme counts only vowel sounds, so that
   ' rode ' may be used as a rhyme for ' goal '. It
   was the original form of rhyme in French, and is
   common in Spanish literature. As a substitute
   for full rhyme it has never become popular in
   English, but it is frequently used for its effect,
   which may be very striking:

   ' Dull, dull and slow
   All motion, as a tale told long ago
   The faded world,'
                    Helen Gray Cone, *The Common Street.*

3. **Cæsura**—The most important pause in a line of
   verse. From the point of view of the reciter its
   use is most effective, particularly in blank verse,
   more so perhaps, than is generally realized.
   Notice the wonderful distribution of the cæsura in
   Tennyson's *Ulysses*:

' The long day wanes:‖the slow moon climbs:‖the
deep

Moans round with many voices.‖Come, my friends,
'Tis not too late to seek a newer world.'

> (This poem, apart from its great beauty, is well worth reading as a study of the use of cæsura.)

4. **Onomatopœia**—The use of words in imitation of the sounds they represent: ' boom ', ' crash ' ' swish ', etc.:

> ' Sing about a bumble-bee
> That tumbled from a lily-bell and grumbled mumblingly,'
> James Whitcomb Riley, *The Brook Song.*

The skilful use by the poet of the various figures of speech—metaphor,[1] personification,[1] and so on—are extremely interesting to study, and should be noted by the student. This will all help to form his taste, and aid his appreciation of literature.

[1]See Appendix.

PROSODY, OR THE LAWS OF VERSIFICATION

These laws are not difficult to understand and master, for, although the hand of Nature is here not clearly apparent, she has, nevertheless, guided their making, for they are based throughout upon the natural and universal appeal of rhythm.

Many of the various forms of metre which were used by the Greek and Latin classical poets are not workable in English, because the basis of their verse was quantity, and the basis of ours is accent. The four which are most successful are:

Iambic metre, ‿ —, consisting of feet of one light and one heavy syllable:

> ' Wherein | all per|fect fruits | do flow.'
> Campion, *Cherry Ripe.*

A single foot is called an Iamb, and it helps in remembering its name to divide it and speak it well stressed: ĭ—ām (the b is mute as a final letter.)

Trochaic metre: — ˘

'Fīrst hĕ | dāncĕd ă | sōlĕmn | mēasŭre

Vēry | slōw ĭn | stēp ănd | gēstŭre.'

Longfellow, *Hiawatha*.

A single foot is a Trochee, and may be remembered in the same way as the iamb, thus: trō—chĕe.

Anapæstic metre consists of feet, ănăpǣsts, of two light syllables and one heavy:

'Bŭt shĕ slēpt— | ănd cŏuld lāugh | ĭn thĕ mōrn|ĭng ăgāin

Ăt thĕ Dōns | ŏf Cāstĭle, | thĕ Hīdăl | gŏs ŏf Spāin.'

E. V. Rieu, *Lullaby for a Naughty Girl*.

Dactylic metre — ˘ ˘ where the name of the metre has to be used as a reminder (Dāctўlĭc), as the foot is called a Dactyl. One heavy syllable and two light:

'Cānnŏn tŏ | lēft ŏf thĕm

Cānnŏn tŏ | rīght ŏf thĕm,'

Tennyson, *The Charge of the Light Brigade*.

Another metre which is coming into fairly general use in English is the **Amphibrachic.** A single foot is an Amphibrach (i.e. short on both sides): ˘ — ˘

'Ŏh, whĕre āre | yŏu gōĭng | tŏ, ăll yŏu | Bĭg Stēamĕrs,

Rudyard Kipling, *Big Steamers*.

To facilitate memorizing, the feet are here tabulated:

iamb ˘ —   trochee — ˘
anapæst ˘ ˘ —   dactyl — ˘ ˘
amphibrach ˘ — ˘

Three feet which often appear as irregularities are:

pyrrhic ˘ ˘   spondee — —
amphimacer — ˘ — (long on both sides).

These are frequently found substituted for feet which correspond with the metre. Obviously, they can be used only in this way. A Pyrrhic or Spondaic metre would not be workable, and this applies, in English, also to Amphimacers.

Lines of verse may consist of varying numbers of feet, thus:

Monometer	one foot
Dimeter	two feet
Trimeter	three feet
Tetrameter	four feet
Pentameter	five feet
Hexameter	six feet
Heptameter	seven feet
Octometer	eight feet.

In learning to scan verse, bear these points in mind:
The line should be read first with strongly marked stressed syllables. Having put in the stress-marks, it is a simple matter to divide the line into feet.

Remember that it is possible for a foot to consist of one heavy, but *not* of one light syllable, or, except as an irregularity in iambic and trochaic metres, of two light syllables. So, if a line has a heavy syllable above the average number, it is not hypermetric (See below). It has a greater number of feet than the other lines. One stressed syllable is absolutely necessary to each foot.

Where the metre of a poem is at all doubtful, it is necessary to decide which rhythm has the preponderance, and to interpret the other feet accordingly, on the principle that poets do not generally vary the main rhythm from

line to line. Beginners are sometimes inclined to scan
each line individually, which results in an extraordinary
lack of cohesion, and is, of course, quite incorrect.

METRICAL IRREGULARITIES

There are certain irregularities which are used by poets
in order to avoid the monotony which may result if verse
be written in absolutely regular, unbroken rhythm. Those
most usually met with are:

Anacrusis—a syllable, or half-foot, prefixed to a line
of trochaic, dactylic and sometimes of amphibrachic,
verse:

> ' So) ĭnnŏcēnt | ārch, ‖ sŏ | cūnnĭng | sīmplĕ,
>
> From bĕ | nēath hĕr | gāthĕrĕd | wīmplĕ '
>
> Tennyson, Lilian.

Trochaic. Anacrusis in first line. Dactylic
substitution in first, and cæsura in second, foot
of first line.

> ' Bŭt) ĭf āny̆|thĭng|hāppĕnĕd | tŏ āll yŏu | Bĭg
>
> Stēamĕrs,
>
> And) sŭppōse yŏu | wĕre wrēcked ŭp | ănd dōwn
>
> thĕ | sălt sēa?ᵛ
>
> Rudyard Kipling, Big Steamers.

Amphibrachic. Anacrusis in both lines.
Catalexis in second line.

Cæsura—in English verse, the principal pause in a
line; a point at which a pause in the sense holds up
the metrical flow. Sometimes, but not always, it is
indicated by a punctuation mark. It is independ-
ent of rhythm and need not coincide with the end
of a foot. Great skill may be shown in its distribution:

' And all | togeth|er leave | their treas|ured room

Some bell-|like eve|ning || when | the may's | in
bloom.'

Edmund Blunden, Almswomen.

Iambic. Spondaic substitution in second foot of second line. Cæsura in third foot of second line.

(The artistic value of the cæsura and the classical cæsura are mentioned elsewhere.)   Page 57 & 66.

Catalexis—a line in trochees, dactyls, or amphibrachs, which is short of a syllable or half-foot at the end, is said to be catalectic:

' Give to | me the | life I | love ᵛ

Let the | lave go | by me.'

Robert Louis Stevenson, The Vagabond.

Trochees.   Catalexis in first line.

Enjambment—the running over, in sense or rhythm of one line of verse into the next:

' Over the | mountains ᵛ

And)over the | waves: ᵛ ᵛ

Under the | fountains ᵛ

And)under the | graves: ᵛ ᵛ

Anonymous, The Great Adventurer.

Dactylic. Enjambment from the first to the second line, and from the third to the fourth. Second and fourth lines Catalectic.

This term is often loosely used where the sense runs on from one line to the next* (*See next page*).

Hypermetric lines are those which have one or two light syllables, above the regular number (Hypermetric—' over the metre '). Initially, in trochaic, dactylic, or amphibrachic verse, the hypermetric syllable may be termed anacrusis. Where it occurs finally, in anapæstic or iambic verse, it is frequently called weak, or feminine ending.

It is often the case, in iambic and trochaic verse, that hypermetric syllables can better be explained as anapæstic or dactylic substitution.

' Ānd ŏn | thĕ pīec|ĕs ōf | thĕ brŏ|kĕn wānd

Wĕre plāced | thĕ hēads | ŏf Ēd|mŭnd Dūke | ŏf

Sōm(ĕrsĕt,

Ănd Wīll|iăm dē | lă Pōle, | fīrst dūke | ŏf Sŭff(ŏlk,
                                    Shakespeare, *Henry VI.*

Iambic.   Second and third lines Hypermetric.

' Yŏu knōw, | wĕ Frēnch | stŏrmĕd Rāt | ĭsbōn:

Ă mīle | ŏr sō | ăwāy

Ŏn ă lĭt|tlĕ mōund | Năpŏl|eōn*

Stōod ŏn | ŏur stŏrm|ĭng dăy.'
                        Browning, *Incident of the French Camp.*

Iambic.   Here the irregularity at the beginning of the third line may be defined either as a hypermetric syllable, or as an anapæstic substitution. A pyrrhic is substituted at the end of this line, and a spondee in the third foot of the first line.   There is an inversion in the first foot of the fourth line.

Inversion—Turning a foot upside-down, so that a trochee appears for an iamb, and vice versa. Inversion is hardly possible in anapæstic or dactylic metre, as it would bring four short syllables together.

' Wēarў | wĭth tōil, | Ĭ hāste | mĕ tō | mў bēd.'
                        Shakespeare, *Sonnet XXVII.*
Iambic.   Inversion in first foot.

Substitution—The use of a foot of quantity which varies from the metre of the verse. Substitution may be used in the following way: a pyrrhic may appear for an iamb or a trochee; a spondee may appear in any measure. Remember that dactyls may never be used with iambs, or trochees with anapæsts. In other words, feet with initial heavy syllables cannot be used with feet of different measure, and initial light syllables. The spondee is the only foot which may be substituted in any metre. Pyrrhics are possible only in two-syllable metres. Where pyrrhic substitution takes place, it is often balanced in the same line by a spondee.

' So through | the green | gloom of | the woods | they
    past,

And iss|uing un|der o|pen heav|ens beheld

A litt|le town | with tow|ers, upon | a rock,'
                     Tennyson, *Enid*.

Iambic. Inversion in third foot of first line. Anapæstic substitution in second and fifth feet of second line, and fourth foot of third line.

' As the Af | rican sun | rose in pur | ple and red.'
                   E. V. Rieu, *The Unicorn*.

Anapæstic. Amphimacer substituted in third foot.

' Betwixt | two bill|ows of | the downs

The lit|tle ham|let lies,

And noth|ing sees | but the | bald crowns

Of the hills, | and the | blue skies.'
             Robert Bridges, *The Winnowers*.

Iambic. Spondaic substitution in second foot of first line. Pyrrhic substituted in third foot of third line, spondee in fourth. The same irregularity occurs in the last two feet of the last line, of which the first foot is an anapæst. (Note that this poem is an excellent example of Ballad Measure. *See* Appendix.)

Truncation—A line with a light syllable missing is truncated. Truncation may be initial, internal, or final, when it may be termed Catalexis (q.v.).

' ˇ ˇ Sāve, | ĭn ă cŏr|ner ă hēap | ŏf drȳ lĕaves.'
         Wordsworth, *Address to a Child.*

Anapæstic. Initial truncation.

' Whĕn āll | thĕ wōrld | ĭs yōung, | ˇ lād.'
         Kinglsey, *When all the World is Young.*

Iambic. Internal truncation in fourth foot.

CLASSICAL METRES

Various classical metres, which cannot easily be used in English, are sometimes attempted by poets, with striking effect. Here is a list of the feet which make up these metres, other than those which are usual in English:

Mollosus — — —	Anti-Bacchic ˇ — —
Tribrach ˇ ˇ ˇ	Bacchic — — ˇ
Antispast ˇ — — ˇ	Ionic *a minore* ˇ ˇ — —
Choriamb — ˇ ˇ —	Ionic *a majore* — — ˇ ˇ

Other feet which appear in Greek and Latin verse are so impossible in English that they have not been included.

The following are examples of well-known Latin, Greek, and French classical metres in English:

Alexandrine. This line of six iambic feet is of French origin, and it has never established itself in English as a continuous metre, though Drayton and Browning used it so. It is found with us fairly frequently in single lines among iambic pentameters:

'Let's see | once more | this say|ing graved | in gold;

Who choos|eth me | shall gain | what man|y

men | desire.'

Shakespeare, *The Merchant of Venice*.

Choriambics were written by Swinburne:

'Large red | lilies of love, | sceptral and tall, |

lovely for eyes | to see;

Thornless | blossoms of love, | full of the sun, |

fruits that were reared | for thee.'

Swinburne, *Choriambics*.

The Hexameter is a line of six feet. The term is generally confined to the staple metre of Greek and Latin Epic, which consists of six-foot lines, always of dactyls and spondees, with occasional final trochees, and to its English imitations. This, however, is merely a matter of custom.

Longfellow's *Evangeline* and *The Children of the Lord's Supper* are in hexameters. Coleridge wrote in this metre, and also Southey and Kinglsey, all in the classical style.

'Up to the | hillside | vines, || and the | pastures |

skirting the | woodland,

Inland the | floods came | yearly; || and | after

the | waters a | monster,'

Kinglsey, *Andromeda*.

(Note the cæsura in the third foot, a feature of the Classical Hexameter.)

Ionic a minore is used by John Masefield in his *Sea
Fever*. Throughout the poem, ionics are mixed
with iambs and anapæsts, but they emerge clearly
in the last line of each verse, and in the following
couplet:

' And the wheel's kick | and the wind's song | and
            the white sail's | shaking,

And a grey mist | on the sea's face | and a grey
    dawn | breaking.'

Sapphics have been tried in English, both seriously
and as a burlesque. Canning's *Needy Knife-
Grinder* is the best known of these burlesque
attempts. The metre should run in three long
lines: trochee, spondee, dactyl, trochee, and then
either a trochee or a spondee; and one short line:
dactyl, and spondee or trochee. Thus:

' Then re|joiced she, | laughing with | love, and |
    scattered

Roses. | awful | roses of |holy | blossom;

Then the | Loves thronged | sadly with | hidden |
    faces

Round Aphro|dite,'

Swinburne, Sapphics.

These, and other metres from Latin, Greek and French
poetry, have been imitated by many of our great poets.
Examples may be found among the works of Tennyson,
Coleridge, and Southey, to name some of the best known
among them. As a rule, they cannot really be regarded
as very successful, for, owing possibly to the lack of spondees
in English, it is difficult to preserve the flow of these metres,
throughout a poem.

CHAPTER VIII

RECITING SELECTIONS IN VERSE AND IN PROSE

' Suit the action to the word, the word to the action.'

THE NECESSITY FOR any study, on the part of the reciter, of the laws which govern verse-making, is a frequently disputed question. But surely, if we think about it for a moment, we shall see that, for the reciter to possess some knowledge of the subject is, if not essential, at any rate, desirable. Lacking such knowledge, how can he give full expression to the beauty of verse? As far as rhythm goes, his natural sense in this direction will serve him up to a point, but beyond that point he is sure to make mistakes.

The two main errors into which the reciter tends to fall, are these: he will either over-stress the rhythm, or else he will try to disregard it altogether, and speak the verse as though it were prose. The remedy in the former case would seem to be for the student to speak prose for a time, until he has learned that, when he recites, he is *saying something*, and not merely making a succession of rhythmical sounds. Then he can apply the lesson to the speaking of verse, and should be able to give true value to the words, which will themselves, to a great extent, help him to overcome the trouble. He must grasp the significance, the living force of words, before he can hope to speak them with true meaning. The speaker who tends to disregard the rhythm does so, very often, through a dread of sounding ' sing-song ' and monotonous. Once the essential difference between prose and verse is pointed out to him, it is generally only a matter of practice for him to learn to give to rhythm its rightful place.

Even if a reciter has a most excellent sense of rhythm,

and neither over- nor under-stresses its value, is this sufficient? For the simplest of verse, regularly written, and free of pitfalls, perhaps it is. But give him verse of irregular and intricate metre, full of substitution, inversion, enjambment, how far then will his instinct serve him? Again, how can he expect, without knowledge of the subject, to give full value to the delicate beauty of assonance, onomatopœia, and all the varied graces which add colour and richness to poetry? He is relying solely upon his instinctive response to the music of verse, and instinct, here as elsewhere, is by no means an infallible guide. It is of the utmost service as a foundation, but it must be reinforced, so to speak, by knowledge. Each aspect of verse—the lyrical, the dramatic, and the narrative—demands its distinctive treatment, and only the skilled reciter, whose art is truly the application of knowledge, can fulfil those demands.

OBSERVANCE OF THE VERSE-PAUSE

Throughout the speaking of verse of whatever type, due observance must be given to the **Pause for effect,** or **Dramatic Pause**. Unless there is grammatical pause, the holding-up at the end of the line should be of the slightest, a particular stress of the rhythm — or rhyme, where one exists — rather than a definite pause. Breath should not be taken in these pauses. Where there is an enjambment, the temptation to ignore the verse-pause is strong, but is so important in its prosodic value, that the student must learn to give it its rightful place. There is sometimes, on the other hand, a tendency to overdo the suspension, and to drop the voice at the end of the line. This will be righted when the line is spoken dwelling upon the last long vowel sound in the line and then proceeding without taking a breath, thus satisfying with the ear rhythmically and the sense intellectually.

Undoubtedly, the delivery of lyrical poetry calls more insistently than that of other forms of verse for some knowledge of the laws of prosody and verse-making generally; and the speaking of blank verse makes claims which are but little less exacting. Attempting to speak his beautifully balanced periods as though they were prose, no doubt makes poor Shakespeare turn in his grave quite as frequently as the sing-song efforts of uncomprehending schoolchildren. To speak Hamlet's soliloquy without regard to its rhythmical beauty, robs it of its majesty, and makes of it but a poor nondescript, neither one thing nor the other. Without marked rhythm it is not verse; with a hint of definite rhythm it is not prose.

And here, please pardon a digression for the sake of a plea in a great and just cause.

If only teachers would not force the master playwright on to children, who, because they cannot understand him (they are so young, how can they be expected to understand?), grow to dislike his very name, and so avoid his work all through their lives. It is possible—in isolated cases it is done—to hold out the study of Shakespeare to children as a reward for good work in other literature, and when the great privilege is attained, to make the plays so enthralling a study, that the children learn a love for them, which they will count in later life among their greatest treasures. If boys and girls are told the story of a play in such a way that they realize that the characters are human; if their attention is drawn to the wonderful, irrepressible fund of humour in the comedies (of course, only the comedies would be used at first); if speeches are paraphrased so that they mean something to the young readers; and, finally, if they are allowed to study the plays by taking it in turn to read, and then to play individual parts—why, the deed is wrought. A band of Shakespeare enthusiasts is born. It is heart-breaking to hear a child cry ' Oh, I hate Shakespeare! I've got to learn this whole page for home-work, and there's no sense in it that I can see! ' Of course he ' hates ' it. It would be a wonder if he didn't. Oh, teachers, you whose opportunities are so great, do please give the children reason to love it instead!

But, to return. The **Lyric,** as its name implies, was originally verse intended to be sung to the music of a lyre— music expressed in terms of words. To-day it has grown to mean something rather different, and that is why it demands so much executively. The lyric is essentially reflective, contemplative, for it is the expression of emotion awakened by the *contemplation* of some person, object, or phenomenon. It depends for its effect upon its perfection of form. It is necessary to paint the picture by words alone, for it is of the mind alone, and only the word which the poet conceived to express his mind, can serve his will.

This almost seems to raise a question as to the suitability of reciting the pure lyric at all. Certainly, if a reciter cannot subjugate his own personality, and prevent its presenting his own mind and not the mind of the poet, it would be best for him to refrain. Everything is in the words. Every word, every irregularity, every comma is of importance. Here the reciter is indeed a mouthpiece. Not an impersonator, but a voice.

Take, for example, that perfect gem among lyrics, Francis Thompson's ' To a Snowflake '. In speaking this little masterpiece, any attempt to add to, or improve upon the effect of the beautifully chosen words by tricks of speech or by gesture, would be simply ludicrous.

By this it is not intended to convey that we should speak the lyric in a monotone, or in an ordinary tone of voice. Words have a life, a living force of their own, and they must be allowed to live. The speaker's voice should take its colour from the words. As we read to ourselves, silently, the words do take that life in our minds. When we speak the lyric, we must neither crush that life by being unimaginative and expressionless, nor distort it by allowing our own personality to shape it.

One cannot but sympathize with the poet who says that all the life is in the words alone, and that any interpretation is unnecessary. To him, that is so. But he is inclined to forget that the minds of an audience may not be so alert to the power of words as is his own, so that here interpretation has its work to do; the work of making the words take life in the minds of others.

There is our aim with regard to the pure lyric. With certain modifications it applies to all verse of a lyrical character. Sometimes we find a narrative told thoughtfully and with noticeable delicacy, in perfect prosodic form. Here, if a reciter feels that he can add to the meaning and penetration of his performance by gesture, by all means let him use it. But he will need to be very sure that he is improving his rendering by so doing.

Narrative Verse is easier. Any one with imagination and appreciation of a story should be able to recite a narrative poem effectively. The rhythm will, as a rule, take care of itself, for any poet worthy the name will couch such a poem in simple and suitable metre. Here, the study of prosody is not a great necessity. But in attempting such recitation, the student will begin to appreciate the value of his knowledge of the laws of modulation, facial expression, and gesture.

To an even greater extent will he find the fruits of his studies to stand him in good stead when he attempts **Dramatic Verse.** The reciter must know how to lead up to climax, to give it every ounce of value; how to hold his audience in suspense until the apex of events is reached. The clearest articulation is needed, for a dramatic situation is often introduced by excited, rapid speech. Lastly, a knowledge of the laws of prosody is of the greatest value in this work, for without it the proper balance between drama and verse may be lost.

Character Study has a place apart, and, to undertake it, a reciter requires very definite gifts. The essentials are a quick ear, an observant eye, and an imitative tongue. For some reason, child studies are, as a rule, more badly presented than most impersonations. One does not often hear French, or Irish, or Cockney recitations in an accent which might hail from goodness-knows-where. It is generally possible to gather what dialect or accent the performer is trying to imitate. But the extraordinary vocal efforts which we are sometimes expected to suffer as being studies of children are simply amazing! A child who produced such sounds should be taken to a throat specialist. Possibly this is because the reciter studies other performers instead of studying children, whereas one who desires to imitate, say, a Yorkshireman, will, if he has no opportunity of talking to a Yorkshireman in the flesh, buy a gramophone record in the required dialect, and learn the accent from that. The would-be impersonator must remember, too, that it is not only accent which he must study. It is, to an equally great extent, inflection and voice-production. The very forward production with palatal r sounds of the West of England, the harsh voice, caused by misplaced resonance, of parts of America, the little upward lilt of Wales, are absolutely characteristic, and must be acquired if a convincing study is to be given. The world around us gives endless opportunities for studying people, and that is what we want. The student of human nature, which every aspiring actor and reciter should be, is never dull. If we keep our wits about us, in trains and in buses, and as we walk the streets, there is our book always open before us, always offering something new; never twice the same.

The link between the reciter's work and that of the actor is more plainly to be seen in character and dramatic work than in speaking verse, but indeed, they are travelling the same road, although on different sides of the way. The chief difference in their work may be summed up in a sentence: the actor demonstrates, the reciter suggests. Juliet on the stage, in fear that the phial she holds will fail her, draws her dagger and lays it near to hand. Juliet on the platform has to make plain to her audience both phial and dagger without material aid. She must suggest other people near her, and properties, furniture, costume; she must so truly live her part, and so plainly visualize them herself, that she conjures them up in the minds of others.

Throughout every branch of his work there is one quality above all others which a reciter must develop by every means in his power—Imagination. Anything similar to many of the situations which a reciter is called upon to portray can very seldom have fallen within his actual experience. We cannot *know* what are the sensations of Othello or Juliet, of Hamlet or Lady Macbeth. Let us take imagination for our tutor.

In dramatic work we learn to imagine the state of mind which is directing each character. Once we can really 'get inside' a part, we shall make no mistakes in characterization. Every movement, every pause and inflection will be in the part. A great actor is said to have remarked that it is impossible to play a part until one is capable of ordering a dinner for the character which one is playing. We need to 'get inside' the character we are trying to introduce to our audience. By a fusing of experience and imagination our own personality is blended with the one which we are for the moment living.

Narrative work demands the same imaginative thoroughness. The reciter should be able to give the impression that the events related did closely concern him, even if he is not recounting his own experiences.

In lyrical work the imagination plays a part more delicate, more poetic, but emphatically no less important. Here we have to imagine and convey the thoughtful emotions of another; to enter into the thoughts and dreams of a poet. This is no easy task for imagination to perform.

INTERPRETATION

The vexed question of the interpretation of verse by the reciter becomes every day more disputed. Some argue that interpretation is unavoidable and vitally necessary; others, that it is a liberty. Verse, the latter school says, is perfect as it stands, perfect in its rhythm and its delicate arrangement of words. It should be spoken in an auto-matic, rhythmical monotone. Tone colour, vocal expression, and of course, to an even greater extent, any form of physical expression are almost sacrilegious.

A factor which has to be dealt with by this latter school is the personality of the reciter. Does the contact between the reciter and his audience depend upon sight, and will it foster the illusion that the voice of the speaker is entirely impersonal, that the sounds it utters are, as it were, merely the printed word become audible, if the reciter is concealed behind a curtain? This again, is a disputable point, since sensitive people are frequently aware of great personalities on the other side of the microphone, without any material evidence. The veiling of a personality is surely no question of vision. It is far more a matter of the reciter closing the imaginative windows of his mind, and speaking verse with his concentration fixed upon its rhythm, and never swerving toward its sense. Otherwise, it is almost impossible for him entirely to cloak his reaction to the power of the words.

As has already been pointed out, words, to the poet, are all-sufficient. Words, rhythmically arranged or not, are to him the summit of beauty—pure, all-sufficing perfection. But for the man in the street words alone are not all-sufficing. Something more is needed to bring home their significance to his consciousness.

The point at issue is really this: Have words a vitality, a life-force of their own, or not? Since all words are, in their origin, onomatopœic, the answer surely is that they have that life. Then we must allow them to live. We must seek the message which the seer has clothed in verse, and speak it with power and with inspired conviction. We cannot be mistaken in believing that the poet in verse, as well as the poet in prose, or colour, or music, has a vision to show to the people. We will seek the vision, and, having found, will hand it on, never crushed, never distorted, but living perfection.

CHAPTER IX

READING ALOUD

READING ALOUD IS a very important and sadly neglected skill. The popularity of reading circles, play-reading clubs, and so on, is growing apace, but their activity is still far too much confined to small groups of people, which seem never to include children. It would be of the greatest value to children to have reading circles connected with school or junior public library, where they could learn to read aloud really well and become familiar, in a most pleasant manner, with great literature.

The old-fashioned rigid distinction between reading and reciting or acting, has died a violent death, and, as is so often the case, the pendulum has swung in the opposite direction. It was said at one time that reading is reading, and reciting is reciting, and that the distinction should be so clear that, even were the performer not seen, the one could never be mistaken for the other. The same rule was, of course, applied to acting. That the reaction against that view is strong may be demonstrated by the following incident. The writer once was present at a play-reading given by an able and gifted amateur company. Two women in the play have a violent quarrel, which ended, on this occasion, in one woman seizing an imaginary bottle and hitting the other one over the head with it. The stricken lady thereupon fell, book in hand, to the ground, where she lay prostrate until the end of the scene. Then, as the reading was given on the floor of a hall, without screens or curtains, she had perforce to get up again in full view of the audience. This seems, perhaps, to be carrying things rather far. Since the imagination of the audience had to provide scenic and lighting effects, costumes and properties, it might very well have done duty a little further, and filled in this most energetic action.

A reader should be capable, without really acting, of giving dramatic effect where it is needed. This, especially where reading at sight is concerned, requires practice, and the student should read aloud for a few minutes each day—to himself, if he cannot get any one to listen to him.

There is no doubt that the lack of expression in much of the reading we hear is caused by the two particular faults which every reader has to overcome. One is to bend the head down to the book, instead of holding both head and book well up. The other is to glue the eyes firmly to the page, and never to look at the audience. The result is, very often, that, the voice being directed into the book, the reader is almost inaudible; and, invariably, that the expression on the face of the reader is lost to the audience. It must be remembered that the most expressive feature is the eyes, so that, even if the head is held up, so that the face can be seen, the habit of fixing the eyes on the book robs the reader of one of his most valuable means of expression. The student has to learn to hold the book easily, and not clasp it to his chest (an attitude beloved of children); also to look up at every convenient pause, and so add emphasis and colour to his reading. It is of course, in many cases, dread of losing the place which makes readers afraid to lift their eyes from the page, and if the following advice is carried out, the trouble will soon be overcome: Always hold the book in the left hand and let the eye travel across the page towards the audience, and return. All other considerations apart, this ensures a good communication with the audience. It will be found after practice in this way that one does not lose the place, but that the eyes return instinctively to the word they left.

Of course, with prepared reading, the difficulties are not nearly so great. By reading a passage through half-a-dozen times one can gain a fair memorization of it, including a mental photograph of the lines as they appear on the page, so that there is no fear of losing the place. The pronunciation of any difficult words can be ascertained, and the whole passage rehearsed with due dramatic and rhythmic effect. It is reading at sight which requires so much care and practice, and here the student may find the following hints helpful:

1. Before commencing to read, glance over the whole passage. It is surprising how much the mind manages to absorb in a single glance. The eyes take in a rough sketch of the paragraph, and the subconscious mind works upon it, so that, whilst lines at the commencement are spoken, lines which follow are being prepared subconsciously.

2. Try always to look ahead when reading, or, should there be any traps, you will straightway fall into them. Tricky pitfalls, like the past and present tense of the word 'read', have been many a reader's undoing.

3. Do not worry about unknown words which may occur in the text. Do your best with them. No man can do more. And you are just as likely as not, to hit on the correct pronunciation. It is important that you make up your mind on that score, or the knowledge that you are approaching some word which you have never seen before will so distress you, that it will spoil the whole performance. A sensible, expressive and intelligent reading is of far greater value that the correct pronunciation of a few lengthy or obscure words. Very often, in reading verse, you will find the rhythm a sure guide to pronunciation.

4. Lastly, do not hurry. Take your time and never get flurried, for undue haste is bound to lead to stumbling, and the mispronunciation of simple words. Once you have commenced to falter, it is difficult to get into your stride again.

For those whose work demands that they should read in public—teachers, clergy, and so on—the study of voice, production, breathing, enunciation, indeed, of the complete subject of elocution, is of the greatest value, which fact appears to be recognized, albeit somewhat tardily, to an increasing extent.

CHAPTER X

CONCLUSION

IT WOULD BE an interesting experiment to ask, of all the thousands who study elocution, one question: ' Why do you study the subject? ' It is almost certain that the majority of answers would deal with learning to recite; a great number would be on the subject of speech in general; and some would reveal the fact that those with whom they originated had glimpsed the beauty and almost overwhelming greatness of the subject, with its absorbing interest and fascination, and the enormously valuable repayment which intelligent and painstaking study will bring.

It seems that hundreds ' learn elocution ' without giving a thought to the benefits which the study and practice bring to them. Even if they become aware of the benefits, it does not occur to them that ' elocution ' is the open-handed goddess who showers such gifts upon her followers.

A satisfactory answer to these questions might run somewhat in this wise:

1. Elocution, or Speech and Drama, is the Art of Perfect Speech. It is, indeed, both Science and Art. Science is ' knowledge ; knowledge reduced to a system '. Art is ' the employment of means to the establishment of some end, directed by knowledge and skill '. In order to speak perfectly, we need some scientific knowledge, and the art to use it. Before I can reach my goal of perfect speech, there are certain scientific facts which I must grasp, for all art depends upon knowledge. To attempt to become a finished speaker without knowledge were to try to make an apple tart without apples— the essential ingredient would be wanting.

By ' perfect speech ' I do not mean pedantic or theatrical speech, for what is unnatural cannot, by any means, be perfect. I mean speech which is beautiful to hear, and which conforms to the standards set up by those who are the qualified and accepted authorities on the subject. And it is even more than that, for the same manner of speech, however perfect, cannot be used for every description of work, so I must learn to be versatile. It will be necessary for me to read extensively, and take an interest in other arts and other subjects; to study human nature, and to keep my eyes open for beauty everywhere, in all its forms, and so to try to broaden my mind and enlarge my mental horizon, for elocution means all this, and more.

2. I learn elocution because the study gives me a wider knowledge of the beautiful in literature, and especially of great poetry; because I gain self-confidence and poise in speaking, not only in public and on the stage, but in social intercourse. I learn because the ability to speak beautifully is an advantage which is within the reach of us all, and which is of the greatest assistance in business, in my school work, or wherever my life's events may take me. Then again, I learn because I realize that the study of voice-production, which entails a knowledge of the correct method of breathing, is undoubtedly a benefit to health, especially to the nervous system, and to the chest and throat; I catch cold far less frequently. My power of memory and capacity for learning benefit tremendously, which alone is worth while. And I learn because it is a joy to give pleasure to others, and I know of no way of entertaining people in which more pleasure can be given, and with less trouble to others in the way of preparation, than by recitations. No instrument is required, no accompaniment, no

platform. Just enough space on which to stand is all I require.

Now that would be a true answer, would it not? We do gain all that, and more, by our study of this great subject, and to those who suffer from any impediment or defect of speech; any nervous disability, or delicacy of the vocal apparatus, the advantage is even greater.

There are, surely, few subjects in which the student may make such rapid strides toward perfection. The very fact of standing up and reciting or reading often acts like magic, and confidence is born with the need of it. Once correct production is mastered, ' New voices for old ' is a cry which tells a daily miracle.

How very greatly is it all worth while!

APPENDIX

GIVING DEFINITIONS OF TECHNICAL TERMS
IN GENERAL USE

See Page

False Vocal Bands .	folds of mucous membrane which protect the vocal bands . .	14
Foot	the unit of verse; that upon which verse moves or runs . . .	60
Galliambic . . .	a classical metre ·	
Glottal Stop . .	the rapid closing and re-opening of the glottis, resulting in a hard attack upon vowel sounds . .	30
Glottis . . .	the laryngeal chink through which air enters the trachea . . .	14
Guttural . . .	pertaining to the throat; i.e., the back of the mouth	
Heroic Verse . .	five-foot iambic verse, rhyming, generally in couplets	
Hendecasyllable .	a line of eleven syllables	
Heptameter . .	a line of seven feet	
Hexameter . . .	a line of six feet	66
Hexasyllable . .	a line of six syllables	
Hiatus	the concurrence of vowel sounds in a word or at the end of one word and the beginning of the next. Sometimes applied to the con-currence of similar consonant sounds	30
Hyperbole . . .	a figure by which things are pre-sented as greater or less than they really are	
	' The English gain two hours a day by clipping their words.'	
	Voltaire.	
Hyper-metric (over the metre)	a line of verse with one or two extra light syllables; an extra short syllable in a line of verse .	62
Iamb	a metrical foot ◡—	
Iambic . . .	the metre composed of iambs; pertaining to an iamb . .	58
Idyll	a narrative poem, domestic in character, often with a romantic or pastoral setting	
Inflection (L. *flexus*, a bending)	the rise and fall of the voice . .	35
Intensity . . .	that tense quality in the voice and manner which conveys emotional stress	43
Intercostal (between-rib)	muscles used in breathing . .	4

88 THE ART OF SPEECH

For some of these definitions I am indebted to: *Higher English* (Campbell); *A Manual of English Prosody* (Saintsbury); *Modern English Metre* (Mayor).

INDEX